100 Guitar TIPS
you should have been told

Music engraving: Cambridge Notation
Music transcription: David Mead
CD production: Phil Hilborne at Widdle Studios, Essex
CD manufacture: GZ Digital Media, Czech Republic

Printed in the United Kingdom by MPG Books, Bodmin

Published by: Sanctuary Publishing Limited, Sanctuary House, 45-53 Sinclair Road, London W14 0NS, United Kingdom

www.sanctuarypublishing.com

Copyright: David Mead, 2000

Cover photographs: © Redferns and Future Publishing

ISBN: 1-86074-295-5

100 Guitar TIPS

you should have been told

DAVID MEAD

Also available by David Mead from Sanctuary Publishing:

Rhythm: A Step By Step Guide To Understanding Rhythm For Guitar
Guitar Workout

ACKNOWLEDGEMENTS

Thanks to…
JS Bach, Lara Croft, Lucy the Mac, Nescafé, the wine makers of the Bordeaux region of France, Sainsbury's microwaveable Indian meals, Moneypenny the fig plant and Tigger the cat. (His memory lives on.)

Special thanks to…
Future Publishing, *Guitar Techniques* magazine, *Guitarist* magazine, Leo Fender (for inventing the Stratocaster), Eric Clapton, the International Guitar Festival (Tom Kerstens and Phil Castang),

Sanctuary Publishing (Jeff Hudson and Penny Braybrooke), Phil Hilborne, Chris Francis, Tim Slater at Peavey, Jamie Humphries at Music Man and Carol, for typing some of this up and reminding me how good Steely Dan are.

Extra special thanks to…
Ken Knussen and Brian Kettle (better friends no man could have), my kids Timothy and Toby for being generally wonderful little people who I'm so happy to have around, and Dr James Cameron for e-mail insanity and a lorra laffs.

BOOK CONTENTS

CD CONTENTS

CD produced, compiled, edited and mastered by Phil Hilborne. Recorded/mixed by Phil Hilborne at WM Studios, Essex, May 2000.

Equipment: David Mead used Peavey and Cornford Amplification, Ernie Ball Guitars and Strings, Palmer Speaker Simulators and Lexicon, Yamaha and Rocktron Effects.

Drum samples were taken from *Burning Grooves*, used under licence from Spectronics. Drum loops by Abe Laboriel, Jr, courtesy of Spectronics' *Burning Grooves*.
Bass playing and additional drum programming/rhythm guitar and jingles by Phil Hilborne. Phil Hilborne uses and endorses PRS Guitars, Picato Strings and Cornford Amplification.
Bonus backing track: © 2000 Phil Hilborne and Jamie Humphries.

"It's not about technique, it's not about what kind of instrument you play or how many strings it's got or how fast you can play or how loud it is or how quiet it is; it's about how it feels and how it makes you feel when you play." **Eric Clapton.**

FOREWORD

You know, it's just possible that guitar tutors may have been getting it wrong for a long time. Music isn't about learning long Greek or Italian names for the obscure noises you can wring out of your guitar. It's not about learning scales that you may or may not ever use, either. So perhaps it's time to shut that dusty attic of academic twaddle and get back to the real world of learning to play, with the absolute minimum bull possible.

Over the years I've talked to hundreds of top names in the guitar world, and I don't think that one of them gave a fig about how their playing might be defined, dissected or analysed. In fact, a common prelude to an interview would often be "Don't ask me anything about modes because I don't know anything about them!"

For ages, as a private tutor and as a teacher at guitar workshops, I've witnessed pupils simply glaze over at the mention of an academic naming regime for what they wanted to learn. It didn't interest them, and neither should it. I deliberately exposed myself to music's weird inner sanctum in the course of becoming a teacher, but I must admit that all it's really done for me is enabled me to communicate better with other teachers. It's been of little or no use onstage, although I suppose that some of the long words have come in useful while playing Scrabble…

So I began to think of a way in whicih all of the flotsam and jetsam of music's more arcane shores could be circumvented in the interests of passing on only the essentials and getting people to play the guitar without burdening them unnecessarily with a whole thesaurus of words to remember. For years I've looked for a method of getting pupils from where they are now to where they want to be in the future, and have finally come around to agreeing with mathematicians in that the shortest route between A and B is a straight line. So let's try to do without all the frills and trimmings and set about learning how to play in the most straightforward manner possible.

I once told myself that I wanted to be able to get through life without ever having either to play golf or to learn exactly what goes on under a car's bonnet. So far I've managed both, and it's not unreasonable to expect that you'd like to learn to play guitar without knowing what goes on under music's bonnet (or learn to play golf). Let's give it a try, shall we?

David Mead
Bath
Spring 2000

THIS BOOK

"I think it would do a lot of good if they actually banned people from practising guitar."
John Etheridge.

If you've had a look at the contents, you'll notice that the meat of this book is split into two basic parts, which deal with the left and right hands separately. I figured that this is the most straightforward user interface I could go for. I mean, what more is there? There's head and heart, of course, and we'll be looking a little bit at both of these slightly more esoteric areas on our way, but actual playing is fundamentally confined to the separate duties performed by the right and left hands. Another assumption or generalisation I've made is that you're pretty much always going to be playing either lead or rhythm guitar (chords or melody lines), and so a direct route into this particular area is to look at how those duties differ specifically and to learn them accordingly.

In order to round things off, I've also included a workshop section, which looks at one of the most perplexing of all subjects on the instrument, that of constructing a solo from the ground floor up. I hope you'll see that this area isn't as frightening as it's often made out to be, and that anyone can put together a proper-enough sounding solo to suit the occasion perfectly. We need to be honest with ourselves and work within our limitations, often turning apparent weaknesses into strengths. We'll cover all of this in the course of the first three sections of the book.

Tagged onto the end, I've offered a few supplementary words of advice and wisdom on the subjects of gear, playing live, turning pro and passing auditions. All of these things are likely to crop up in your own playing life. I mean, it would be a pity to confine your new-found skills to the bedroom for the rest of your life, wouldn't it? I'm hoping that you'll feel suitably confident and inspired to want to play in a band, or at the very least with a group of friends. Like it or not, you're performing every time you pick up a guitar in front of anyone. It doesn't matter if it's a few mates down the pub or a few thousand people in an arena, performance is performance and you need to be prepared for it.

We'll touch on the somewhat obscure area of improvisation, too. This is an area which contains more fear than just about any other for the average guitar student. I'll try and prove to you that you improvise every day in one way or another, and that learning to do so musically and with a guitar in your hand isn't really such a hard trick to master.

Lastly, I'd like to make a deal with you: I promise that I'll keep all of the unnecessary, jargon-encrusted patois out of this book in return for your promise that you'll give all of the various exercises, programmes and tasks your best shot, at the very least. We'll keep the hard slog down to an absolute minimum, but it's up to you to do the necessary work, and I guarantee that we'll make you into the best guitarist that you can possibly be.

INTO THE LEARNING ZONE

"You never can learn enough with any instrument. I don't practice as much as I used to, but when I was really into my late teens and early 20s I kept a guitar by the bed with the radio turned down real low. Nobody would hear it except me, and every time a guitar would come on and you'd hear something, you'd grab the damned guitar right then and get as near to what you heard as you can. If you could sleep with that guitar in your hand it wouldn't be too much guitar. Yeah, you need to fool with that thing as often as you can and as long as you can, and if you love it like I do you would be one of the best. Spend as much time with it as you can, *more* than you can, even though you know you've got to put it down sometime. Every chance you get you put that damned thing in your hand and you fool with it!" **Buddy Guy.**

People learn at different rates. It's something which every teacher has to recognise and cater for – or at least *should* recognise and cater for. Something very useful for a student of the guitar to assimilate at an early stage is his or her own personal learning pattern. We all have them; there comes a point at which, no matter how much you practice a song, idea, lick or phrase, it just doesn't get any better. You hit a brick wall and seem to stop dead. What's happened is that the mind has switched of, and you've become stale. The learning facility in your brain has shut up shop and found something better with which to occupy its time. You might be going through the motions with your hands but your head is busy thinking about football, television, gardening or some other activity a hundred miles away from chords and scales. The solution to this problem is to realise that it's happening and not be defeated by it, to remember that it happens to all of us, and to put down the guitar and go and do something else. The most important thing to do is not to feel downgraded or depressed about it. Consider it all as being part of your own personal learning cycle. It's only natural, so deal with it.

A lot of the time you can make your practice time more efficient by stopping just before things start to get stale and getting on with something else. This is far more rewarding. Look at it this way: if things aren't getting any better because your mind has started to wander, you'll be able to return to the task of learning a bit later on, and you'll be coming back to it fresher and better prepared. By recognising the human tendency to suffer from boredom, you'll have turned a minus into a plus, and you'll have beaten the system a little, so don't beat yourself up for no reason. Take it as part of guitar-related human nature.

The "Can't Do" Barrier

Every teacher knows that a pupil's greatest enemy is the "can't do" barrier. It stalks the corridors of learning like a spectre, waiting in the shadows, ready to jump out and intimidate the unwary student. Your most important weapon in the fight against the "can't do" beast is your own self-confidence and ingenuity. If something seems impossible at first, there is always a good reason why. Maybe you're not sufficiently technically prepared and need a very simple regimen of exercises to build up extra stamina. Maybe you need to take another look at an area of your technique and make some refinements. These are things which a good teacher will help you to recognise early on and help you to deal with.

However, if you've decided to go it alone and teach yourself, you'll have to learn to be your own teacher, counsellor and guitar buddy. You'll have to imagine that you can see yourself in the mirror at all times, ready to jump in and offer advice, encouragement and suggestions for improvement. Most of all, you'll have to keep your own morale in check. Don't become disheartened if something isn't working out. Tell yourself that many other guitarists have been down this road and found solutions to the problems you're encountering, have beaten the "can't do" barrier and have gone onto the next stage. You can do it, too. It takes time, patience and the ability to focus on a set of short-term objectives. Don't set yourself Herculean tasks and then wonder why you can't achieve instant results. (We've got a name for this syndrome, too – see below.) Instead, celebrate every step that you take on your way to becoming a better musician, no matter how small they may be.

Personal Everests

Another of the problems which a guitar student practically invents for himself I call "personal Everests". These are the goals a student will set himself which are so far ahead in terms of his rate of development that he is sure to fail from the word go. This is another blight on the early development – or even later development – which can bring your progress grinding to a halt unless you're careful. I have seen this syndrome many, many times and always do my utmost to halt it before it took too much of an effect. A personal Everest is a goal that a pupil sets for himself with a timescale that just isn't possible. You could call it running before you can walk, but seeing as there always seems to be a lofty height involved with a true personal Everest, I dubbed it that.

Case History

I once had a student who came to his first lesson with a Steve Vai music book under his arm and a criminally out-of-tune guitar in his hand. He had high hopes in his head, too. I spent the whole hour trying to tell him that he had set his sights too high and that there was a lot of work to be done at base camp before he donned his climbing gear and set off to conquer Mount Vai. A couple of years later, I told Steve Vai this story and he said: "And the kid didn't come back, right?" Steve was right, he didn't stay the course, having fallen victim to his own personal Everest.

The secret of progress is the setting of short-term goals. This is where a lot of self-discipline will spare you a lot of disappointment. Short-term, reachable objectives will guarantee progress, but if you try and take quantum leaps then more often than not you'll find yourself falling flat on your face. If this form of discipline seems unnatural to you, and you don't think that you can trust yourself to take tiny steps, then in all likelihood you need the tender ministrations of a teacher, someone who will tend and encourage you along the way and steer you away from the north-face fantasies of the personal Everest syndrome.

It's really just a matter of pacing yourself. If you try to move too far too fast you'll find that your development as a guitarist is very adversely affected. Consider someone who wants to eventually run a marathon: no one would think that they could just get up out of an armchair and run 26 miles if the most that they had previously achieved was occasionally running for a bus. In fact, such a thing would be physically impossible; your body would actually make you stop when it started running out of vital resources, and you would end up a breathless lump on the pavement. Unfortunately, given that guitar playing physically doesn't have the same draining effects, there isn't that natural fuse which blows and tells us that our ideas are impractical.

You must pace your development on the guitar in the same way that you would approach running a marathon, slowly and surely. There's nothing wrong with having great plans for the future, in the same way that you could train yourself to run 26 miles after, say, twelve months without needing an ambulance. The idea itself is fine, but actually doing it straight away – or even the next weekend – is out of the question.

We'll delve further into the avoidance of impractical targets later in the book, but for now just think how much easier it's going to be to achieve your objectives on the guitar in small but manageable steps.

The Three Ps

The three Ps stand for Patience, Persistence and Practice, and these three words should become something of a mantra as you make progress. In reality, every obstacle that the guitar – or music in general – throws in your path can be overcome by sensible administering of the three Ps. Sadly, the exact opposite seems to be the case in many students – they apply the practise of impatient, occasional twiddling to solve their problems and it simply doesn't work. You think I haven't tried?

Anyone attempting to learn any musical instrument is prone to all kinds of frustrations, but it always seems to be the stoical approach that works best and offers more positive results. I've known players who have tried for hours to master some little nuance of style in a doggedly determined, focused and completely non-distractable way. Some people think that this kind of quiet dedication is unnatural or strange, but it generally pays off.

Achieving this kind of goal – that of competence on a musical instrument – is open to much misunderstanding, and you can count yourself blessed if the people in your life understand your aims and goals and allow you the space in which to achieve them. When the going gets tough (and it will, occasionally – just remember the three Ps), it's quite a good stress-buster!

READING TABLATURE

"Maybe 10% have been readers, but the rest of them all had to learn it like a parrot."
Frank Zappa, on employing musicians who could read music.

In a number of ways, tablature has been a life saver for the modern guitar student. In itself, it's an easy enough system to learn – I've proved to pupils on many occasions that it takes little more than an evening to become familiar with the basic ins and outs of reading guitar tab, whereas it takes considerably longer to learn how to read standard notation or "proper" written music.

I'm often asked by pupils if I think it's necessary for them to learn to read music, or even if I deem it essential. I always reply that it depends on what you intend to do with your guitar playing. If you aim to turn professional and want to channel your endeavours into becoming a session musician then reading skills will be of considerable advantage to you. Also, if you want to enter any field in which reading music is involved then of course you should learn. However, the simple truth is that many students want to play for their own pleasure, or maybe with a few friends, and for this the ability to read music is far from necessary. I often add that, even though I don't consider it necessary in some cases, if they still want to learn to read music then it's no problem. I believe in a flexible approach towards teaching and in serving the needs of any pupils who come my way as best I can, after all.

"A lot of the time we write the way any other band would write, just in a rehearsal, playing off one another; but it does help if there's a complex arrangement, whether rhythmically or melodically, and you can write it out and give it to the other guy. Or, if the keyboard player is going to double something I'm going to do, I can just write it out instead of sitting there going through it note by note." **John Petrucci** (Dream Theater).

So, to put the whole thing in a nutshell, it's necessary to learn to read music if you're ever going to place yourself in a situation where reading is the norm, or if you badly want to learn for some other reason. Other than that, it's not necessary.

These days, it's pretty much accepted that reading tablature is the way to go if you're learning to play. I believe that it's over used in many ways, though; it can become a substitute for a guitarist learning to use his ears, and that's a bad thing. It's like an art student being content to paint by numbers and never learning to paint by observing nature. By relying entirely on tablature, you're only seeing half of the picture. You will only ever learn to reproduce, never create, and that's not a good thing.

"Showing somebody how to play something is very shallow…The thing you want to show them is how you get it, how you invent things on your own." **Steve Vai.**

Used in moderation, tab is a great system for communicating material from which a student can learn. When I'm taking a lesson I nearly always write a solo out in tab rather than standard notation, and I often feel that it's my duty to get the pupil into the ball park and leave it up to him to fine tune what he has learned himself, using his ears. This balance is essential, I feel, in order to make sure that a reliance on tablature doesn't stifle any creative process which is native within the pupil himself. If he relies on tab, I believe that he will remain incomplete as an effective musician.

So Let's Learn How

Having said all that, I'm now going to teach you how to read tab!

This system of guitar notation has been around for about 400 years or so. It began at around the time that the guitar's ancestor, the lute, was in fashion and started life as a notational system which was dedicated and exclusive to the instrument. This was both an advantage and the factor which lead to tab's eventual downfall, because it wasn't a system which would readily transfer to any other instrument. Falling by the wayside in this way, guitar music was then brought under the nurturing influence of standard notation, a system which was universal to all instruments.

Tab made a re-appearance relatively recently, but it was considered to be a poor second to the more adaptable system of standard notation. During the Eighties, tablature once again dominated the field of guitar music. The wealth of music for guitar which became available was quite staggering, and no doubt helped tab to find its way into the hearts of a whole new generation of players. It was also buoyed up by the rise to fame of guitar heroes like Vai, Satriani and Malmsteen, whose influence caused guitar sales to peak at levels that they hadn't seen since the beat boom of the Sixties.

Far from being a cop out, tab established itself as a valuable learning tool. However, as I have said, I believe that it has replaced a lot of necessary skills, such as basic ear training, to the detriment of guitar playing in general. So we're not going to get hooked here, are we? We're going to use it as a source of reference and learn to build a connection between the ears, brain and hands.

The Basics

Realistically, all you need to know about tab is that the six lines shown below represent the six strings of the guitar, with the bass E string at the bottom.

Exercise 1

TRACK 2

The system which shows you where to put your fingers really couldn't be simpler. If you study the next example, you'll notice the number eight on the bass string.

Exercise 2

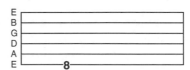

This means that you play the note which is located at the eighth fret on the E string, which is a C. In order to notate solos or melody lines, tab looks like this:

Exercise 3

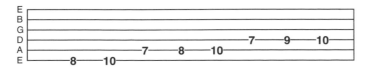

The tab is read from left to right and the numbers (ie fret locations) are played in sequence. If you are expected to play more than one note at a time, the notation will look like this:

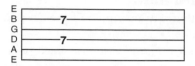

Treat these stacked notes as one basic musical event, as you would a strummed chord. Talking of chords, they would look like this:

Exercise 5

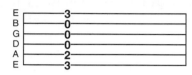

Exercise 6

That's the chord of G major, which might look a little more familiar in the form of a chord box:

You can see that the principles of tab and chord boxes are extremely similar, and they're also extremely straightforward. We've already covered the basics; the system is merely expanded to encompass whole songs, solos and rhythm parts.

You might have spotted what I believe to be tab's greatest drawback: it's all numbers. It's as musical as playing a bank statement, and just about as creative – in its basic state – as painting by numbers. There's no rhythmic information, nothing to tell you how long a note lasts or the ratio in length between one note and the next. It's an incomplete system, musically speaking; it doesn't give you the whole picture, by any means, and to use it exclusively or to become dependent upon it would be to condemn yourself to remaining blinkered for life.

Tell yourself right here and now that you won't become its slave. Use tab as a reference and a guide, nothing more. Being incapable of playing anything without the tab in front of you is like never taking off your water wings when you want to venture out into the middle of the pool by yourself. You're missing out on a hell of a lot by remaining tethered to it.

In order to make the information in this book as immediate as possible, I've included only tab and no standard notation. This is only because I want everyone to be able to access the information without encountering much of a problem. I'm not inviting you to adopt a system for life!

THE DOCTOR IS IN!

"It's very important to listen. Listen and learn from other players, but also put yourself in a position where you can listen to yourself." **Joe Satriani.**

One of the most useful things that you can do as a student of the guitar is to diagnose your own problems. It's a fact that you're going to run into quite a few, especially at first, and so training yourself to diagnose problems – and possibly even prescribe treatment – is a very handy ability to have. To this end, I'm going to tell you how to earn yourself a medical degree in guitar-problem analysis in about 3,000 words. You're probably only about 30 minutes away from qualifying, so get yourself comfortable.

Musical Or Physical?

Over the many years that I've spent dealing with guitar players at all levels of competence, I've figured out that there are really only two types of problem that people bring to me: *musical* or *physical*. If they are unable to do something with the instrument, time and time again it would fall under one or other of the above headings. By being able to file a problem away under one of them, you're a lot closer to dealing with it, because usually the remedies are pretty similar.

The body has to adapt itself to the various unnatural acts which the guitar demands of it. Take a good look at anyone's playing position and you'll probably agree that much of what he or she is doing is outside the body's usual sphere of activity. There's the position of the left hand, for instance. Doing all of that delicate manoeuvring with the wrist in that position isn't normal; the body has to be trained to adapt itself to perform that way. When you take into account all of the special muscular development that has to take place in order to play, you can see where a great many problems

lie. If the thumb on your left hand hasn't developed the necessary muscles to cope with barre chords, for instance, you're going to find that kind of action difficult, right? It's therefore not a musical problem as such, it's a physical one, and by filing it in its proper place it can be dealt with by good old-fashioned practice – that is, the type of practice that will target the problem and solve it for you.

A musical problem would be something like a student coming to me and saying that, while he could hear really great guitar music in his head and could play competent versions of other people's tunes and solos, he failed to connect with his own original voice. That's to say that his technique was pretty much together, but he lacked the basic ability to channel his own ideas through to his hands.

Beginning to get the idea? At guitar seminars, I quite often write these two headers on the board, *physical* and *musical*, and then I ask the students to name me some problems that they've been experiencing while learning to play. I tell them that it can be anything they like, no matter if they consider it too insignificant to mention under normal circumstances. The list I get is quite often very similar from seminar to seminar. I'll hear things like "I can't use my left-hand little finger too well", and I'll write that under *physical*. I might hear "All of my licks sound the same – I'm getting stale", and I'll write that one under *musical*. After just a little while, I can generally hear pennies dropping all around the classroom as the assembled throng begins to recognise the division between the two areas. We might end up with a list like this:

Musical	Physical
I lack originality	*My barre chords stink!*
I can't work out solos by ear	*My picking is sloppy*
I can't hear if something's right or not	*I can't stretch far enough*
I don't know which chords go together	*I've got no independent movement between my third and fourth fingers*

Soon enough, everyone starts to get quite excited to think that their basic problem areas can be so efficiently catalogued – and, of course, they look to me for some quick fixes. In actual fact, most of the problems grouped under the *physical* header can be sorted out with some sort of gradually progressive practice routine – the key is nearly always practice. The *musical* column is usually also dealt with by fairly simple remedies; quite often it's down to training the ear.

Musical problems are nearly always related to the amount of general music awareness that a student has gained while learning, and this could be referred to as his ability to speak the language of music. How fluent is he? It's the same thing as going on holiday to a foreign country and having to rely on a phrase book to get by. You're only as good as your memory, pronunciation and wits will allow. Left to your own devices, you might order the wrong thing in a restaurant, ask for a foil-wrapped armadillo instead of some sun-tan cream, or insult the hotel staff quite unintentionally. When you think about it, this is the sort of thing that happens if someone's basic musical fluency isn't up to scratch: a lot of the things you play are inappropriate or just plain wrong, you experience problems remembering things you've learned and, well, nothing really flows, does it? Do you see the similarities? I hope so, because the solutions are very similar.

It should be obvious why we can't get by with a phrase book when playing music; we need to operate on a much less casual and more fluent manner in order to function more efficiently. With this in mind, if you were faced with the situation where you had to make yourself understood more consistently and interact conversationally with the natives, what sort of measures would you take? You might enroll in some sort of night class to learn the language more comprehensively, or you might decide to jump in at the deep end and stay in the country, where you would quite literally either sink or swim. Either way, a lot of your learning would be based on your ability to listen and imitate, and it's the same with music. There's more to it than just listening to a lot of music, too – you also have to have some sort of plan in order to get inside the basic "language" and learn from it.

Some wise man once said that "most people merely look, but only the artist really sees", and I think that we can apply this to music. Most people listen, but only the musician really hears. It's definitely not enough to listen – it doesn't go far enough. Listening to the voice track of a foreign movie doesn't teach you the language; you have to interact on a far more fundamental level. It all comes down to seeing the process of basic musicality as something of a cycle: hearing, understanding and playing. If your learning is confined to "phrase book" practices – reading a solo in tablature but never being able to remember it afterwards, for instance – then the job is only being half done. The piece isn't being heard or understood, and so it can't possibly be of any use. We're back to using a phrase book again.

If it sounds like this particular set of problems (filed under the *musical* heading) is going to be difficult to beat, you're wrong…in a way. They can be dealt with in a very similar way to the problems classified as *physical*, it's just that you're dealing with mental muscle this time, not physical. It might be harder to imagine yourself developing in this intangible area, but it's a trick that I have personally taught a lot of people, and I've seen the magic begin to work countless times.

The first thing that you have to do is learn to vocalise what you're listening to. Getting someone to sing what they play always pays dividends, as it starts to build the bridge between what's going on in the head and what's happening on the guitar fretboard. If I have one rule in this department it's simply this: if you can hum it you should be able to play it. With the notes in your head, you should be able to find them on the fretboard. Part of Joe Satriani's learning programme with the great jazz pianist Lennie Tristano was that he had to learn to sing solos note for note:

> "One thing I learned from Lennie Tristano was singing other people's solos. A lot of people like to emulate solos by copying them, but his trip was to put on a record and sing the melody and sing the improvisation.
>
> "When I was studying be-bop with Lennie, it was more of an organised challenge because those guys played notes; they didn't have wang bars, distortion, feedback and stuff which is difficult to sing. But I'd sit there and put on a record and go 'Do-bap-da-deedly-ah-dee-bah', or whatever, and just follow it, and he would demand that I nail it note for note.
>
> "So I would spend all week learning the solo note for note – not on the instrument, but with my voice. He was interested in the student absorbing or digesting the music coming from the soloist, and I guess that he thought that, almost in a visceral sense, you would learn it and know it in a very personal way, rather than just reading it on manuscript and saying 'Oh yeah, look, he used a minor third over this' and trying to emulate it. Plus he realised that a lot of his students couldn't possibly play Charlie Parker solos. When I first met him, I didn't have the technique on guitar, but he knew that my voice could imitate it and he thought that was a very important key to getting the student to understand where music comes from – it comes from inside, not from the instrument." **Joe Satriani.**

This facility helps you in countless ways, one of which is the ability to work out solos from records. The process is always the same: hear it, hum it, play it. The guitarist Mike Keneally, who used to play with Frank Zappa and now tours with Steve Vai, also expounds this simple philosophy:

> "I just became good at isolating tiny little blasts of music and figuring out the component parts. If I heard *du-du-dah* I could easily process that as three separate notes and figure out what the notes were. You just break it down into tiny, tiny chunks. For some reason, I would never put the thing on tape and learn it that way; I just kept putting the needle back on the vinyl – and wore out a lot of needles!" **Mike Keneally**.

This process of learning to tie up the different functions of hearing and playing can be started easily: try to play anything that you can already hum. If I tell 20 people to give this a go, I can usually bet on at least 18 falling into the old "personal Everest" trap of being too ambitious. They'll try to play something that they only *think* they know. You've got to know a tune really well before it's possible for you to be able to reproduce it on the guitar, and this is why I advise people to start off with nursery rhymes or children's songs. The chances are that these tunes have been engraved on their consciousness at a time when their brains were wide open to every learning experience available to them, and the result is that they know them really well.

Experiencing the difference between knowing something and merely thinking that you know something is quite simple. Try this experiment: hum a tune from your nursery years. It can be anything, but make it simple and well known. If you need a few suggestions, 'Three Blind Mice', 'Happy Birthday To You', 'Twinkle Twinkle Little Star' or 'John Brown's Body' are the sort of songs I mean. Anyone trying Bartok's *Concerto For Orchestra* is disqualified. Hum whichever melody you've chosen and then pick up a guitar and hum the tune again, one note at a time. Every time you hum a note, try to find it on the guitar. Keep humming the note and wait until you find that pitch on the guitar. Then hum the next note, and the next, and so on.

If you experienced problems with this task – and I expect that a lot of people did – then you can see the path in front of you. You can't expect to tackle anything more elaborate until the link between your ear and your hands is established, and there's a straightforward way in which you can start to do this. The secret is in daily repetition, whilst being constantly mindful of the three Ps: Patience, Persistence and Practice. Try a different tune every day, or even the same one every day, although I would suggest introducing as much variation as you can muster. You're not teaching yourself how to play the melody to 'Happy Birthday', or whatever; you're teaching the brain a little trick of co-ordination. You're beginning a very vital process which will serve you well in your musical endeavours from this point on.

Solo Endeavours

Of course, there will be some of you who found stage one relatively simple but who are still mystified as to why they can't work out guitar solos from records. Well, remember what I said about "knowing" a tune a moment ago? Take a moment to repeat the mantra "If I can hum it I can play it", and then see if you can actually hum what you're trying to learn. In cases where guitar students experience trouble when learning something from a record, 99% of the time it's because they don't actually know the tune well enough to hum it first. The music's not in their heads, and so how can it possibly be in their hands? Believe me, this is the problem in a nutshell, and it's a problem which forms the best part of many a guitarist's largest stumbling block. We'll be dealing more with this later in the book, so don't fear; we're far from finished with learning melodies from outside sources.

Students often say to me that they can't actually hear some of the notes in a part or solo, that they can get most of the notes but that there are just one or two which somehow remain out of reach. If this has happened to you, don't worry; these notes don't reside in the twilight zone, it's just that your basic vocabulary hasn't incorporated them before. You just haven't been introduced, that's all – you're still strangers. More experimentation will lead you towards being able to hear them in your head, and being able to hum them without a problem – it's down to the three Ps again. Once you've begun to be introduced to these strangers, it will get easier and easier. Remember that there are only twelve notes to learn, but that's still seven more than a lot of guitarists seem to be prepared to cope with.

Mixing With Strangers

So how do we set about becoming intimate with these strangers, exactly? Believe it or not, it's a job which can evolve all by itself, if approached strategically enough. For a start, you're going to have a go at humming things you play when you practice, right? If you're playing a few chords, take the time to sing each note in each chord individually. It doesn't matter if you feel self-conscious – if it embarrasses you, make sure that you're well away from everyone first. Hum each note of every chord, and make sure you do a little bit every day. Then try the hum-and-play routine, using simple melodies. Once you can do this to a fairly satisfactory level, provide yourself with new input: find a solo that you really want to learn. Remember, though, nothing too adventurous too soon. If you're still a little wobbly on your feet in this area, make sure that you attempt only short, slowish melodies that you can pick out on the record. No personal Everests, please!

The next step is to leave the guitar alone and just try to hum the notes you're trying to learn. This is best accomplished by trying to hum very short bursts to begin with, and the chances are that initially three or four notes will be your maximum. Any more than this and you'll be asking a bit much. Once you're able to hum a phrase with confidence – and only then – pick up the guitar and give it a try. By now your explorations with nursery rhymes should have cleared the way for you to do this, but don't get frustrated and give up at the "can't do" barrier. Even experienced transcribers sometimes have to play a passage 20 or 30 times before they get it right. The point is that the link between head and hand is beginning to develop, and things can only get better.

Tone Deaf? Probably Not

While we're on the subject, I'd better clear up another point which crops up from time to time. I've had so many pupils say to me "I think I'm tone deaf", but I have honestly never met anyone who wants to learn to play the guitar who is tone deaf. The fact that they enjoy music means that they have a "feel" for it, and what these people mean is that they have an ear which is currently undeveloped, that's all.

Any ear can be developed to focus on the language of music and to become a valuable asset. All it takes is a combination of the things we're trying to achieve in this book: abandoning personal Everests, observance of the three Ps and learning to laugh in the face of the "can't do" barrier.

> "I just listened to it. I developed a pretty good ear, although I started out as a complete idiot." Joe Satriani.

TRACKS 3-12

In order to help you out a bit with the task of learning to develop your ear-to-hand co-ordination, on the CD I've included a little experiment I used to conduct with pupils. This is what happens: I play a note on my guitar and you find it on yours. In order to make the job a little easier, I'm going to give you some clues to help you along. For a start, I'm going to tell you the string on which I'm playing the note, and I'm only going to play notes that are between frets one and twelve. In this way, you've got a one in twelve chance of being right, even if you shoot blindly in the dark. But the rule is this: listen, hum, find.

When I've tried this experiment live in lessons, a lot of students have been surprised at how close they can get after only one or two tries. Your ear will quickly determine the parameters for which it's being asked to scan. One hint is to spend a bit of time playing the notes between frets one and twelve before attempting the test; in this way you'll give your ear a few vital landmarks in advance.

After spending a while on individual strings, the area which you have to search will become broader, and the notes that you have to find will be on the lower or upper three strings. Even so, the system for solving each of the puzzles remains the same: listen, hum, find.

All of this is explained on the CD, and I really would encourage you to give this one a go. The students I've introduced to this test have all benefited from it, and it will help you to take a few more steps towards your goal of total confidence with the instrument.

SO WHY PLAY GUITAR?

"I got my first Gibson for £80. It was a Les Paul Special, a cherry one…
God, I loved that guitar." **Mark Knopfler**.

Well, that's why we're here, isn't it? Everyone has their reasons for picking up the instrument in the first place, and I thought that we'd look at a few case histories from some of the guys who have provided quotes for this book before we start all of the fun and games of actually learning anything.

For my own part, I can't remember why I started learning. Well, not really. I know I went through years of wanting a guitar desperately. Every birthday and Christmas was a period of high expectation and subsequent disappointment until I was taken over to a guitar shop in Kingston and was bought a cheap nylon-stringed acoustic just to shut me up. Rumour has it that this was the same shop that had sold Eric Clapton his first guitar a decade or so earlier, but we'd better let that one pass, I guess.

At this time I was listening to The Beatles, The Beach Boys and…erm…The Bonzo Dog Doo-Dah Band. I didn't know it then, but I was about to be introduced to Frank Zappa and Cream, and that did it. I can remember hearing track one on side one of *Goodbye Cream* and thinking "What's going on?" It didn't make any sense in the context of what I'd been learning, which had been confined to folky-type chordal stuff. However, it must have triggered something because the electric guitar was then a beast that I wanted to tame and a puzzle that I somehow needed to solve.

I think it was probably a single phrase on the track 'Sleepy Time Time', on Cream's *Live Cream* album, which convinced me that I wanted to play guitar professionally. It was the second of Clapton's unaccompanied lead breaks in the middle of the song, and I can remember thinking then that I had to learn how to make a guitar

sound just as powerful and as majestic. My parents thought that I was mad, and tried everything they could think of to make me change my mind, but I was sold into the slavery of learning guitar and nothing was enough to buy my freedom!

If my parents thought that I was mad then I don't know what they'd have made of Mark Knopfler's habit of sniffing Fender catalogues as a kid. "They had a smell of their own," he told me. Hmmm…

Other players came to the instrument in different ways.

"My father had a guitar which he kept in a closet, but I never played that. I didn't really decide to mess around with the thing until we got this awful thing at an auction… it was an archtop, f-hole, ugly motherfucker with the strings about half an inch off the fretboard. I liked it because it was so tinny sounding. It was just an acoustic guitar, but…it was moving closer to the direction of that wiry tone I liked with Johnny 'Guitar' Watson." **Frank Zappa.**

"When I was six I took guitar lessons and gave up the guitar because the first thing the guy did was show me how to read, and started to teach me notes and music theory, which had nothing to do with playing guitar. I would do an enormous amount of work on the maths of music without the reward of hearing something back that I liked. After a month of lessons I could maybe play the first few notes of a nursery rhyme, whereas I wanted to play a bit of rock 'n' roll, which he probably could have shown me just as easily." **Paul Gilbert.**

Every musician to whom I've spoken has one thing in common: they took up the guitar in response to the prevailing music of the time and a need to somehow get involved.

"I got a Kay double cutaway. I got one because Alexis Korner had one…Anybody who had an idea of how to play any instrument could just about hold their own [in the Sixties] because there was no competition – there was no one around…If you could play anything in a halfway-convincing fashion, you were the boss, and there were so few of us…I was so deadly serious about what I was doing – I thought everyone else was either in it just to be on Top Of The Pops *or* Ready, Steady, Go! *or to score girls or for some dodgy reason. I was in it to save the fucking world!"* **Eric Clapton.**

"I started playing the guitar in my lap when I was about 18, but in 1980, on my way to the recording studio for my fist session of my first album, I was a passenger in a Volkswagen and we got hit head-on by an American police car and I broke my back. Basically, I was out of commission for about a year, and during that time I was obliged to wear this horrible metal cage around my torso to keep me straight. Every time I tried to play guitar the cage would scratch it up, and so that's when I really put my energy into playing lap-style because I could still play that way. I figure that the accident was God's way of telling me to practice more before recording." **Bob Brozman.**

"My father talked me into it. I actually wanted to be an illustrator – I wanted to draw – so I would come home from school every day and do my homework, then listen to music and just draw. My father thought I was too serious about my schoolwork and wanted to find something that would make me more social! He had a friend who played guitar with Tommy Dorsey and Paul Anka and he gave lessons, and so I started playing. I don't think there would be too many kids whose parents worry that they're too much into their schoolwork!" **Reeves Gabrels.**

"I always had a very eclectic musical palette. Everything from mainstream radio – you know,

Stax and Motown – to Skip James. And for me, it was natural that it reflected itself in my performing. But the trick was getting it to the point where it wasn't just playing musical ping pong; it was something more cohesive." **Eric Bibb.**

"I had a few lessons, but it didn't last very long and so I ended up being self-taught. The guy I was taking lessons from was self-taught, and so he told me that I should just do what he did and teach myself, because by the time I started lessons I was pretty far along. I was just getting him to show me licks and teach me songs and stuff, so he said 'Well, I can show you a few things, but you should just play all the time and show yourself.'" **Warren Haynes** (The Allman Brothers).

"I started playing when I was a kid, about twelve or 13. I was living with my step-father and my mother, and it was my step-father who taught me how to play. He gave me a guitar called a Stella. The stuff I'm playing now, that's his style." **John Lee Hooker.**

"My first guide was my uncle, who was a great guitarist and accordionist. He used to play all these lovely waltzes and tangos – dancing music, but with a great European melody. I think I learned a lot about structure, songs and melody then. It was a very formative time for me." **Antonio Forcione.**

"The way I learned is that I plunked my fingers down into a chord shape, listened to it. If it sounded good then I did a mirror image of it, and if that sounded good then great. That's got to be your only criteria: does it sound good?" **Bob Brozman.**

"I used to skip school and paint my face with Ace Frehley Kiss make-up. My dad got me my first guitar and I started dicking around with it, learned how to make a barre chord, discovered feedback and that was the end of it. No formal lessons or training…just listening to records and picking up on licks and stuff." **Dimebag Darrell.**

"I tried working out all the Barney Kessell Trio solos when I was about 16." **Andy Summers.**

"I was at music college, studying classical guitar, but then I thought: 'Fuck this, I want to get into a band and get a Strat!'" **Dominic Miller.**

"My initial guitar playing stuff came out of folk music…My scale of interest was incredibly broad: folk music through blues and through to straight pop music. I wouldn't say that blues was the dominant one." **David Gilmour.**

"I got involved in folk music because I couldn't afford an amplifier, and so I couldn't be in a beat group, although I desperately wanted to be." **Mark Knopfler.**

"My main influence was Eric Clapton, then Buddy Guy, Elmore James, Jimmy Reed and John Lee Hooker – although not for his guitar playing. More his songs." **Peter Green.**

"I had a daily half-hour routine, and my father told me not to wiggle my thumb and to keep my fingers in position." **John Williams.**

"The general answer I give, often to earnest and well-educated interviewers looking very serious with their books of Nietzsche behind them on the bookshelf, is that it's the best way I know to make a lot of noise with one guitar." **Robert Fripp**, on the creation of *Soundscapes*.

However, for whatever reason you've chosen to try and solve the riddle of how to wring the soul out of a guitar, we're probably all united in one thing:

"I liked the way it sounded." **Frank Zappa.**

Amen to that, Frank!

RHYTHM

"I love anybody who plays a good groove. All the James Brown stuff, I think it's brilliant. As a player, I don't like to be conspicuous; I don't think being conspicuous is an essential part of guitar playing." **David Rhodes.**

I've said it before and I'll say it again: the popular conception of a rhythm guitarist is that of a slightly inferior musician playing a subordinate role to a lead player (who is often possessed of an ego the size of Mars). And yet, playing rhythm – defined as being strictly chordal and other sundry harmonic duties – is what we all end up doing for more than 80% of an average gig. Nearly every song has a rhythm part, and yet a sense of rhythm is so often a yawning gap in any guitarist's basic vocabulary. So let's try and put matters right, shall we?

Maybe it's the words "rhythm guitarist" which are themselves the nub of the problem. Perhaps we should redefine things right here and now

and refer to the act of playing chords and such as "harmony guitar" or "accompaniment", or whatever it takes to get the average guitarist to sit up and listen, I guess. However, let me say one thing once and for all: you're going to be playing a lot of rhythm when you play guitar, so please pay attention to this area of your playing. Getting this part of your musical life sorted now is going to save you a lot of grief later on because, yes, rhythm is as important to lead playing as it is to…erm…accompaniment. So listen up because this is important, and it's so easy to overlook if you have never had a rhythm player's role explained to you properly before.

THE RIGHT HAND

"People always make fun of me because I can't pick the 'proper' way." **Edward Van Halen.**

This is the hand which either holds a pick, or at any rate strikes the strings, right? If you've elected to play the guitar left handed – and you've really made a burden for yourself if you have – then you'll need to reverse things here.

The first thing we need to talk about with the right hand is the subject of plectrums (or plectra, if you did Greek at school). These simple pieces of plastic are probably the cheapest pieces of gear you'll ever buy, and yet they can make an incredible difference to your playing. It's therefore worth a moment or two of your time to study its role.

So many times I've been able to put a pupil back on the right path by suggesting that they change their pick.

Case Histories

I once taught someone who was frustrated at the fact that he could play scales against a metronome reasonably fast but, when he tried to play them above a certain speed, his accuracy went completely to pieces. I couldn't understand it, and for that matter neither could he. During one lesson, I decided to take a good look at his right hand to see exactly what was going on and what could possibly be holding him back. As it turned out, he was functioning correctly as far as his right hand was concerned, but he was experiencing the equivalent of becoming tongue tied when the beats per minute got beyond a certain level. In desperation, I asked to take a look at his pick. It was one of those fairly large triangular affairs which are all well and good – I know for a fact that Buddy Guy uses one, for example – but it obviously didn't suit this particular guitar player because once I suggested that he tried something a little smaller he was off. His accuracy increased by about 50%, and all because of

something which probably cost him a few pence in a guitar shop.

At a recent guitar seminar, I encountered one pupil who was playing so softly that you could hardly hear him. I was going around the class getting the students to play a twelve-bar solo over a blues riff just to get them settled in and used to playing together. When it was this particular guy's turn, the overall volume dropped. There was practically no dynamic information in his playing, although his actual choice of notes was really quite good. When I spoke to him during a break, he said it was because the pick-up on his guitar was a low-output humbucker, and it just didn't cut through enough. Now, I know an excuse when I hear one, and so I told him that this couldn't be the case because the older Gibson guitars – especially those of the much-revered and sought-after '58 vintage – had very weak pick-ups when compared to today's humbuckers, so it had to be something else. In order to prove my theory, I took his guitar from him and played a couple of licks on it myself. It sounded great...and the dynamic level went up by 85%. I looked at his pick and, sure enough, it was a flimsy .44m, which would be better suited for strumming folk acoustic than it would be for playing down-home blues. When I substituted a more manly plectrum for his weedy one, his tone and dynamics instantly improved. Once again, the solution was about 50 pence's worth of plastic.

Flash The Plastic

The advice with regard to plectrums is to experiment with a few different shapes and sizes. Be aware that they come in different thicknesses, too. I can't predict which thickness is going to be right for you, but I can tell you that the majority of rock and blues players tend to use fairly hefty plectrums. By hefty, I mean around .80mm-1mm thick. To put it another way, they don't show an awful lot of bendiness if flexed between the fingers – they're pretty rigid. When used on the guitar, this translates into giving the strings a pretty solid clout with almost no flexibility on the part of the pick.

Taken to the extreme, some players use absolutely rigid metal plectrums – or, in the case of Queen's Brian May, an old sixpence:

> "It is heavy, but I hold it lightly to compensate. What I like is that I can feel the movement and it all gets transmitted to the fingers. To me, it's a very sensitive way of playing." **Brian May.**

Of course, ultimately you might find yourself using either a slightly heavier or lighter pick. I'm just telling you what the majority of guitarists use, which is probably a reasonable starting point in your plectrum research.

> "Albert [Collins] played with his thumb and forefinger, which actually led me to use a heavier pick, and sometimes I'd play with my fingers as well." **Gary Moore.**

You might even elect to use your fingers. When confronted with a player who uses his fingers instead of a plectrum, I usually ask them why they made the decision in the first place. If the answer is "because that's what Jeff Beck or Mark Knopfler does" then I give them some gentle counselling and implore them to act like an individual and at least try using a pick like the rest of us before making any decisions which could impair their ability unnecessarily. If I get the answer that they've tried using a pick but they honestly get on better with their fingers, and can prove this to me in some significant fashion, I let it pass with a warning that they might find that some things might be more difficult to them than they are for the rest of us. I also advise them that it might be a good idea if they adopted the ideal *adapt to survive*.

So you're going to visit a guitar store and buy a few different-sized picks just to make sure that

you're optimising your right-hand abilities as soon as possible, right? An investment of about £1 (or the international equivalent thereof) is well worth your trouble, believe me.

Strings Attached

While we're at it, do you know what gauge strings you're using? Can you remember the last time you changed them? I ask because strings are another comparatively cheap piece of gear which influences a guitarist's sound and general sensibilities enormously, and yet it's an area which is so easily overlooked.

To give you an example of how important strings can be, you can be sure that at every concert you've attended the guitarist has been using a fresh set of strings. Changing their employer's strings before every gig is one of a guitar tech's most laborious tasks. So why do you think changing them is so important? Well, it's easy to forget that new strings sound different to worn strings. It's because we get used to our guitar sounding duller and duller as time goes by – it happens so slowly that we don't even notice. New (or relatively new) strings sound fab, on the other hand, and it's new strings that you hear at every gig and on every record you've ever bought, so bear in mind that a new set might just give you that extra tone and sustain that you think you've been missing.

Gauge

So what gauge strings *do* you use? This is the punchline of many musician jokes (although I prefer the one that ends with "So what sort of sticks do you use?"), but it's another of those often-overlooked aspects of guitar playing. If I were to offer a few facts and figures about strings, I might point out that the default (ie the most popular) gauge is .009mm-.042mm. Don't ask me why, it just is, OK?

I'm sure that you don't want to hear a history of string manufacture from me (we're keeping waffle down to a minimum, remember?), but if you're curious I'm sure that there are web sites aplenty on the internet which a few minutes' toil with a search engine would produce in abundance.

But can string gauge really be that influential to a player's sound? Well, yes it can. What's more, it's another of those relatively modestly-priced variables in the guitar player's arsenal, and so it would seem silly not to give it at least a few moments' thought. If I can distract you for a moment with a few lines about physics (nothing too involved, so fear not), strings vibrating in a pick-up's magnetic field produce a small current, which is then amplified and delivered to the audience as a guitar note. With me so far? The more metal which is actually set in motion, the higher the signal will be, making the job of the amp and the pick-up a little easier. A bi-product of this feat of electromagnetics is that a slightly better tone is also produced. Maybe it's because subtle nuances like finger vibrato and such are more easily transferred, I honestly don't know, or care too much. After all, if I'd wanted to be a scientist I would have invented something marvellous, patented it and retired to Malibu by now.

I would therefore advise you to experiment at least a little with string gauges. If you increase the weight of your strings by one gauge you might not actually notice that much more strain while bending strings, but you may notice a slight improvement in general tone, which would definitely be worth having.

Don't go mad, though. Increasing your strings from a set of .009s to a set of .012s is not advised. Like everything, moderation is a very good thing.

Case History

I once had a pupil who found it impossible to bend a note in tune. He'd try his best, but would always go way too far, and the resulting sharp note was painful for both of us. I suggested that he upgraded his string gauge, believing that the extra resistance offered by the slightly thicker strings might keep his wild over-bending in check. He changed from .009s to a set of .010s and bingo! No more out-of-tune bends. It cost him about £5 to sort out the bug in his playing. I guess that the moral of this particular story is that, when you think you've got a glitch in your playing technique, sometimes it's actually a hardware problem – just sometimes.

One final point about strings. When my pupils are ready to change strings for the first time, I usually recommended that they watch me do it for them. Over the years, I must have changed strings on my guitars thousands of times, and I can pretty much do it in my sleep. What's more, I've seen the pros do it (guitar techs and guitar repairers), and so I'm pretty sure that I'm doing it right. There are things you can do here which will give you tuning instability and other sundry nightmares, and so if you're not sure you should ask someone who you trust to show you the ropes. It could save you that little bit of irritation in the long run.

The Quirk Factor

OK, so we've got a plectrum with which we're relatively happy. Now all we have to do is check that we're holding the thing in such a way that it won't hold us back from playing well. It's a slightly depressing fact that, in the world of holding picks, practically anything goes, so I'd like to introduce you to something that became familiar to all my pupils: the Quirk Factor. The Quirk Factor states that, no matter what advice I give you, you'll go out and find someone who appears to be having a great time doing exactly the opposite! This can result in me swearing blind that I've shown you the best possible way of playing something – all of the right notes and all of the the right chords – even though you've seen the artist who played the original in concert performing it differently. In this case, I would hope that the notes are the same, and that he's probably just playing it in a different position on the neck of the guitar.

The Quirk Factor can be a real pain because it does seem to contradict even the best and longest-considered advice that you've received from an apparently informed source. I don't introduce it as an escape clause in the spoken contract I have with the people who come to me for help, but it's necessary to introduce it as an explanation of why sometimes I appear to get things wrong. So if, after reading this particular section, you go to a gig and witness someone playing totally competently by holding their pick between thumb and little finger, remember the Quirk Factor. All I can reasonably promise you is that I'm telling you how 98% of the guitar-playing world go about doing things. There are always one or two mavericks in any walk of life, aren't there?

Talking of 'Walk Of Life', we have to consider the choice of players like Mark Knopfler and Jeff Beck, and many more, who opt to play using their fingers. There are a couple of unique styles brought about, at least in part, by the decision to play with flesh rather than plastic.

Case History

I once had a pupil who came to me for lessons in jazz playing. He was interested in the chord-melody approach to playing, which suggests to me a finger technique in the manner of the great jazz guitar virtuosi Joe Pass and Martin Taylor, although my pupil seemed happy to play with a pick. I didn't want to contradict this because players like Barney Kessell employed a perfectly respectable chord-melody technique while using a pick. Both sound different, but each approach is perfectly acceptable. However, he seemed to be experiencing some difficulty, and so during one session I suggested that he tried playing with his fingers instead. He looked at me in disbelief and told me that his former teacher had never let him play with his fingers, despite the fact that he personally felt that his progress might be enhanced by doing so. He put down his pick, and I don't think I ever saw him with one again. He had made the decision himself, based on trying both approaches, and he found the right one for him. His former teacher was very wrong to give him a distorted view of the pick or fingers debate.

The moral is that sometimes a style of music carries with it certain protocols with regards to technique, and a little bit of self examination (and an open-minded teacher) is called for before progress can be assured.

Holding The Pick

By far the most common technique for holding the pick is between the index finger and the thumb. There is a tendency for some people to want to support the plectrum with the middle finger, too, but in general I would advise against this. What you want in your right hand is freedom of movement, above and beyond everything else. This means that you must rid your hands of public enemy number one: tension. It stands to reason that, if you're asking your hand to perform some fairly athletic moves, the last thing you want is anything which snags that basic freedom of movement. Tension can

show up in different ways, and can have damaging consequences in the long run. An awful lot of repetitive strain injuries are caused by unwanted tension and restricted movement. You therefore need to adopt a basic picking stance which will mean that you've got the most opportunity to remain relaxed and efficient. This means two things which might be considered as being golden rules:

1. You should only need to use your index finger and your thumb in order to produce speed and efficiency. Anything more might feel comfortable now but will possibly hold you back later.

2. Don't form a fist with your right hand. Instead, imagine that you're going to need continuous access to your guitar's controls. An "open-hand" approach is going to help a lot in this department.

Why not a fist? The answer is down to tension again. The act of keeping your hand closed or fingers bunched up means that muscles are being used for something that isn't directly concerned with playing the guitar. Right? You don't need any unnecessary distractions from the rest of your body when you're trying to play.

"If you stiffen up, you lose the groove." **Jeff Tamelier** (Tower Of Power).

It makes sense, but watch out. Here come a couple of examples of the Quirk Factor at work…

You might have seen Eddie Van Halen play guitar close up, and if so you may have noticed that he holds the pick between his thumb and his *second* finger, and you might have thought that he certainly didn't have any apparent problems rewriting the book of guitar playing in the late Seventies by doing things this way. True. All I can offer in the form of a rebuttal is that God knows how he makes it work, but he does. However, it probably won't work for you! All the odds are stacked against you if you try things this way. Just nod your head sagely and mutter: 'Aha…the Quirk Factor."

Secondly, returning to Dire Straits' guitarist for a moment, consider the question of tension in the picking hand. Have you noticed the way in which Knopfler anchors his fingers to the face of the guitar while playing? If I try this, it produces immediate discomfort and considerable loss in freedom of movement, but it works for him and that's fine. It's the Quirk Factor at work again, contradicting guitar tutors worldwide in its own little unhelpful way.

Anchor Points

While we're talking about anchoring our picking hands, it's fairly common to rest the picking hand somehow. The exact method you use will come with experience. Here's what Joe Satriani has to say on the subject:

> "I came upon this position which I eventually settled upon where you anchor your hand with a couple of fingertips on the body of the guitar." **Joe Satriani.**

Trial and error reigns supreme in many areas of playing guitar. Once again, I'll repeat that all I can do is tell you what the majority of guitar players do. Only time and experience will teach you any personal variations that you may have to make in order to get the best out of your playing.

Basically, it's necessary to anchor your hand somehow in order to enable the right hand to orientate itself with the strings irrespective of the guitar's position. The fingers need a few landmarks so that they know where they are. Don't imagine that your fingers have to be fixed to the front of the guitar with superglue, as this would introduce tension again. A light, relaxed "dusting" of the fingertips, which will allow for the occasional grope in the direction of the volume and tone controls, should be all that is necessary. The minute that you sense that your hand is in any way restricted, go back to the start and try again. It's worth it in the long run.

Los Angles

> "Altering the angle of your pick will produce different sounds and I recommend that you experiment in this area, too." **Joe Satriani.**

Once you've clutched the pick in your sweaty little hand, it would be nice to think that the job's nearly over and that you can get some actual playing sorted out, but there's one more question to cover, and it concerns angles.

It might be tempting to think that holding the pick so that it's flat on to the strings would be all that is necessary to get the job of picking well under way, but it's not quite as simple as that. As your (relaxed) hand passes over the strings, it describes an arc, much the same as those that appear in algebra text books. This means that the pick is never really going to be "flat on" to the strings, even if it should start out this way. This is another occasion when I can report that the rank and file hold their picks so that they are slightly on edge to the strings. Therefore, given a starting position on your bass E string (ie the one nearest you), you should find that the pick attacks the string initially "edge on" – that is, that the left-hand side of the pick hits the string first. This is a popular technique amongst guitarists. Many claim that this picking stance actually gives their playing an edge – and I'm sure that there was no pun intended.

Allowing for the Quirk Factor, you're going to find players who contradict what I've just said, but if we consider again that we're dealing with the majority of players and their picking habits then once again the advice is that you adopt this picking technique for now and refine it later should circumstances insist.

Now that you've got a suitable plectrum, a good picking angle, a fresh set of strings and a good, relaxed playing position for your right hand, it might be a good idea to look at some of the duties this hand is expected to perform in the pursuit of good, solid rhythm technique.

THE LEFT HAND

"Rhythm has always been my thing. When I used to listen to records,
I used to listen to the drummer." **Malcolm Young** (AC/DC).

So what exactly is the left hand's role in all of this rhythm business? If you can imagine that your right hand is the conductor, and that it's that hand's job to perform the bulk of your rhythmic definition, then you can easily consider the fingers on your left hand as the gentlemen of the orchestra.

Obviously, the left hand's fingers take on the role of forming chords and, like the right hand, it has to be fairly limber in order to do so. Chord changes can come thick and fast in some musical moments, and so you should expect to undertake something of a training session for the left hand at some point.

The most common complaint from students who are encountering chord changes in the early stages are these:

"My fingers don't want to go where I put them"
"I keep fluffing notes within a chord"
"I can't change chords quickly enough"
"I can't find the best hand position"

Let's deal with these problems one at a time. Incidentally, if you've just said to yourself that all of these problems should be filed under *physical* in our doctor's consulting room, award yourself a few extra points.

"My fingers don't want to go where I put them"

Well, nobody's fingers want to go where you want them to go to begin with, and if this sounds like you then let's smash through this particular "can't do" barrier straight away. One of the reasons why the digits on your left hand are being obstinate and unco-operative is really quite simple to understand: you're probably right handed, and your left hand just isn't used to being asked to perform anything too dexterous. Think about it; what do you do with your left hand in general? I expect that it's not a lot at all – you've trained it to change gear in the car perhaps, or answer the phone, but fingering an E major chord is a far more delicate job, and so if your left hand is slow to respond don't become frustrated with it. With practice, it will soon pick up the necessary skills and you'll be able to play pretty much anything you want with it.

If you want me to suggest a training programme in this respect, I would recommend sitting in front of a sheet of chords (you could use the one on pages 38-9 in this book if you wish) and playing them in a different order every day. That's it, nothing more. Limit yourself to about ten minutes of this particular exercise per day and you're practically guaranteed results. The secrets here are:

1. Recognise the problem as a physical one – ie you require some sort of physical training plan.

2. Address the problem with a set of exercises that you perform daily within a limited period of time.

3. Be patient and don't expect immediate results

4. No personal Everests!

The rules and regulations regarding playing chords are covered in the chapter entitled (spookily enough) 'Learning Chords'.

"I keep fluffing notes within a chord"

This is down to hand position. It's as simple as that. What's happening, without much doubt, is that one or maybe two of your fingers are snagging on the adjoining strings. If you sense that you're not playing with a full deck with any chord – that is to say that you sense that there may be a couple of strings which are coming out with a *blmppph* instead of a note – then try playing the strings one at a time until you find the culprit and then take a good long look at your hand/finger position. You should be able to see the problem (it will be apparent that a finger is lying against another string and muting it), and correcting it will be only a few moments away. With a little bit of repositioning, you should find that the problem cures itself. However, don't stop there – you have to make your hand remember how you solved the problem, and so it's vital that you repeat the process several times.

There is such a thing as finger memory. I had this proved to me a number of times during the time I took classical guitar lessons. I was occasionally coming up with awkward chord shapes (classical guitar music is full of them), and if he sensed I was having trouble my teacher would make me stop, hold the chord and repeat the placing of my fingers several times over in order that my fingers learned the move. It's a bit like ballet (no, seriously!); you can't expect to be able to perform these delicate changes of position and placement of your fingers the first time, every time. You have to choreograph things and teach your little team of digital dancers to remember all of the moves. As you progress, they'll learn more quickly because many of the moves that seem new and strange now will feel like variations on a theme – and therefore more familiar – later on.

Don't be content to repeat mistakes. If something's wrong, deal with it immediately. You'll love yourself for doing so later on.

"I can't change chords quickly enough"

Once again, nobody can do this at first, and everything I've said about "can't do" barriers applies here. When you change between chords, you're asking the left hand to perform some delicate aerial ballet moves. (Later on we'll see that chord changes take place in mid air and never on the fretboard.) They need some training before they can work safely without a net.

The exercise I mentioned a couple of paragraphs ago is going to help here, too. By going through a chart of chords in a different order every night, you'll soon pick up the necessary chord-changing skills that you'll need. Once again, the secret is Patience, Persistence and Practice.

If you find that it's maybe one particular chord change that is causing you grief, turn it into an exercise. Don't let it live within a piece of music as a mistake (it will, if you don't correct it now); tell yourself that you'll deal with it. Isolate it and practise it separately. Keep a little red book of problem areas and look at it every time you sit down to practice. Call it *Work In Progress* or something. If these little things are addressed on a daily basis, your progress is practically assured.

If you want a tip or two, consider this: a chord change is like a journey. It has a point of departure and a destination, and your problem lies in the space between: the journey itself. One basic piece of good advice is therefore to take a good look at your journey between these two points. Are your fingers performing the move in the most economical way? Are you wasting energy by involving fingers which aren't actually needed for the destination chord? Is there a note common to both chords where a simple re-fingering could mean that you're saving yourself the job of actually moving that particular digit?

It's the consideration of points like these that will help you overcome any specific chord-changing problems, because they're things that an experienced teacher would look for. By training yourself to deal open-mindedly with these little glitches, you're helping yourself to become more independent with the instrument.

"I can't find the best hand position"

The best hand position is the one which works best for you! Sorry to be so vague, but it's true. Everyone has slightly different-sized hands, fingers and so on, and so an ideal hand position has to be found. There can't realistically be one and only one that works when you acknowledge all of the variables that are present in the equation. However, here are some guidelines:

1. Your thumb should take on the role of aiding the support of the guitar neck, which should be quite secure in the V formed by the thumb and index finger on your left hand. If you tip the guitar away from you, it's your fingers that stop it from slipping further. Similarly, if you tip the guitar backwards, it's the thumb's job to make sure that the neck doesn't slip out of your hand.

2. It's only classical guitarists who have to keep their thumbs in the middle of the back of the neck, and this is due to the position which this form of guitar playing demands. Take a look at a few pictures of classical guitarists and the "thumb rule" should make sense. Rock players don't hold the guitar in the same way, and so the thumb peeking over the top of the neck is not just allowed, it's positively encouraged.

3. Your thumb can act as a fine anchor point for carrying out techniques such as bending. In fact, for this – and for other, similar techniques – hooking the thumb over the top of the neck is highly recommended.

4. As far as your thumb is concerned, the cardinal sin is to lay it down in the direction of the guitar's headstock so that it's semi-horizontal. In this position, the thumb's isn't performing its primary function of supporting the fingers and offering stability to the guitar neck. You wouldn't try to pick up a book and hold it like that, and the same applies for guitar playing.

After a while, your playing position will become established and will begin to feel completely natural. However, my advice would be to keep it under constant review. Just because you've become settled with something doesn't make it right, and a lot can be achieved by demonstrating a willingness to keep an open mind and be adaptable. Old habits, as they say, die hard.

LEARNING CHORDS

"After I'd been in it quite a while, it struck me rather forcibly that I knew sod all about music and what I would have to do really would be to learn a little bit about it…So I thought I'd try to figure out a little more about it, that's all. So I just sat down and made myself stick at it…It wasn't easy, but then it just started becoming easier and easier and I realised that even if I couldn't always remember the name of something, then I would recognise the sound. It's like learning a language where you don't know the long words but after a while you recognise them, like a child. So now I say 'That's a 13th with a flattened ninth' because I recognise the sound." **Mark Knopfler.**

I suppose that rhythm guitar is synonymous with playing chords; it's almost certainly the first thing you think of, and learning chords is one of the guitarist's earliest nightmares.

The main reason for this is largely down to the chord books you find in music stores. They've got titles like *10,000 Chords For Guitar*, and the would-be guitarist grimaces but buys the books anyway. In truth, it's a bit easier than that.

My way of looking at chords is to learn them in the right order, and by that I mean to concentrate on the ones that you need to know and leave the more elaborate ones until much later on. Too many guitar students make the mistake of treating a chord book like a tutor and trying to learn from it accordingly. This is wrong. If you buy a chord book – and it's a handy thing to have – then tell yourself that you're going to use it like a dictionary and look up the odd chord if you need to. Don't be fooled into believing that you will ever need all of them. (Incidentally, a little later Joe Satriani will tell us all that he treated a chord book as a form of tutor. Remember what I said about the Quirk Factor and just smile and nod when this happens, OK?)

So if we're going to look at learning chords in the most economical way possible, how are we going to go about it? To start with, you need a tad of information from me. Don't worry, there are no long names to bother with here. Listen up and I could save you an awful lot of time and trouble.

Let's look at a few facts. Music is music. It doesn't matter whether it's country, rock, pop, metal or blues, it conforms to a set of basic rules.

It comes as a surprise to some people to hear that, in terms of chords, there's very little difference between a rock song and an orchestral piece. It always sounds like there's an awful lot going on in an orchestra – the arrangement of instrumentation and so on will be more involved than just you or me strumming a guitar – but basic principles are at work in both cases and some surprising similarities exist. (Incidentally, I hate the word "strumming", but I can't think of a better one and so it will have to suffice for now.)

The fact is that chords exist in every kind of music, and a lot of the time they're the same chords. There's nothing fancy about a classical or orchestral chord. An orchestral chord is going to sound different because of the instrumentation involved; it's got nothing to do with actual notes.

I sometimes ask students how many notes there are in an average chord on the guitar. Many will say six because that's how many strings they've got. If I ask how many notes they think there is in a piano chord, they'll often shrug and pick a number between five and ten (they often regard ten as being the limit owing to how many fingers they've got). Most chords actually contain only three notes, irrespective of whether they're played by a guitar, piano or symphony orchestra. The reason why this is so is all to do with that area of music theory with which I promised not to worry you – just a brief demonstration will be all that's needed. If you want to know more, there are books that can tell you.

Let's consider the chord of C major. It's quite often one of the first chords we learn and so I'm assuming that it will be familiar to all of you. Down at the nut of the guitar, it looks like this:

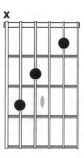

From a theoretical point of view, the chord of C major contains these three notes:

C E G

The chord above contains these notes:

C E G C E

See what's happening? All we've done is repeated a couple of the notes. It's still a three-note chord, and so it would be if it were played on any instrument. If it didn't contain those notes, or if it contained more notes than those I've mentioned, you'd be playing something different and it would have a different name. Just to hammer the point home, let's look at another chord shape for C major:

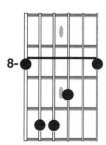

This one is the barre version for C major that you play at the eighth fret. It's a six string chord this time, whereas the one before was five, but if we look at what's going on in terms of actual notes, we get the same result as before:

C G C E G C

It's the same three notes, just mixed in a slightly different way this time.

Now that we've got this fact under our collective belts, it's time for another. Most music is made up from very basic chords. We can make a song arrangement as complicated as you like, putting in all sorts of fancy chords along the way, but stripped down to the bare essentials most songs use very basic chords. So if you were trying to put together a game plan for learning chords, you'd learn the basic ones first, right?

All the way through this book, I'm going to try to tell you the right order in which to learn things, and as far as chords are concerned things couldn't be more simple.

Ready for another fact? Chords can be split into three basic groups: major, minor and seventh chords. Don't worry about why they've been given the names they have – words just describe a sound, remember? The only difference between these three groups is how they sound. Let's take our chord of C again. If you play these three C chords one at a time and listen, you should be able to hear a difference between them.

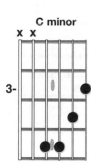

Start with C major and try to think of how it sounds to you. It sounds positive, happy and quite at rest. By that I mean that it doesn't sound like it needs another chord to follow it immediately or anything.

Now try the C minor chord. It's a bit different isn't it? This time, it sounds more sad, unhappy and certainly less final than the major version before it.

Now play the third chord, C7. Does it sound unfinished to you? Like it really needs something after it to finish it off?

If you can hear these differences, well done.

You've taken an important step in learning to hear music and spot some very basic details about chords. If you didn't hear too much of a difference the first time, don't give up. Keep coming back to this exercise and, as your ear begins to develop, you'll start to hear this fundamental difference between the main three chord groups.

Now, believe it or not, a very large chunk of music can be played with these three chord types. Sure, you might have sneaked a look towards the back of a chord book and found chords with names like Cm7♭5 or G7♯9 and other horrors like them, but I repeat: you can play a very large chunk of music knowing only the chords from these three groups. All of those other chords can wait for a while. If we want to cover the most distance in the shortest time, let's look at how we can make learning chords as easy as possible.

Given that information above, it follows that our first job is to make sure that we know all of the basic chords, right? Well yes, that's absolutely right, as it happens. Just to spell things out once and for all, you have to know the following chords:

A major	**A minor**	**A7**
B major	**B minor**	**B7**
C major	**C minor**	**C7**
D major	**D minor**	**D7**
E major	**E minor**	**E7**
F major	**F minor**	**F7**
G major	**G minor**	**G7**

Here's a chord chart to use as a guide or checklist:

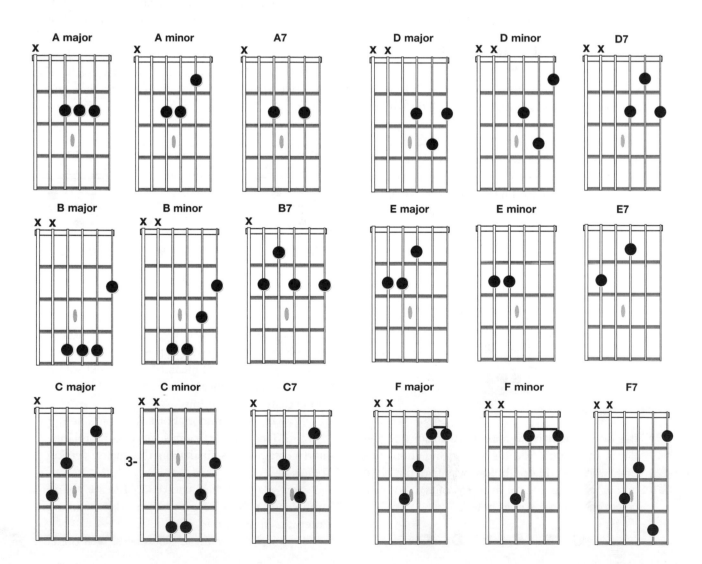

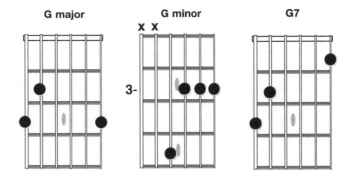

You may now be thinking that these particular chords aren't really the whole story, and you'd be right. There are some more chord names, which have things like flat or sharp signs in their titles. Happily, I believe that there is a way to accommodate these slightly more difficult blighters at a stroke, and that is by learning barre chords as early as you can. However, don't allow yourself to think that the chords you learn down at the nut (sometimes called "first-position" chords) aren't useful. They are the mainstay of riff-orientated bands like AC/DC, for instance.

> "The quality there is the thing. They're big chords and they can ring for ages."
> **Malcolm Young.**

In order to demonstrate how this can make your life a lot easier, consider these three diagrams:

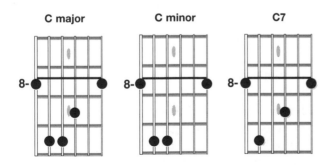

There's one chord for each of the groups we've been looking at. You'll notice that each involves laying the first finger right across the fretboard and laying other fingers down to the right of it. This is our first joust with Mother Nature, and it's difficult. Our fingers were not designed to

do this. Our muscles aren't ready for us to try to do this either, and so we've got to understand one thing: learning barre chords will take a little time. It's common sense; suppleness doesn't happen immediately, and muscle growth and development doesn't happen over night. Remember the "can't do" barrier? This is an early hurdle for guitar students and one at which it's very tempting to invoke those terrible words: "I can't do it!" But hey, the rest of us can, and all of us struggled with it to begin with, and so you will be able to do it soon, too. Then you'll look back and wonder what all the fuss was about.

You may wonder why barre chords are so important to learn. Well, if I told you that the three shapes we looked at a moment ago are the only ones you have to learn for now because they're – wait for it – moveable, then I trust you're already nodding in agreement and that you've made the decision to buy me a pint at some time.

Moveable Shapes

Barre chords are a splendid way of building up a vocabulary. If you check out any concert videos that you might have lying around, you'll probably see that most guitarists use some form of moveable shape pretty much all the time. Remember, we're not talking about anything too cerebral here. Let's look at the facts once again: most music uses very basic harmony most of the time. A very large percentage of music is harmonised – or accompanied by – chords from one of three distinct family groups. You can play most of them by using a very few shapes.

Now, doesn't that take some of the pain out of learning chords? No wonder so many guitarists are perplexed at the sight of mammoth chord books on the shelves of a music store. This way round, the job shouldn't seem half as bad. So how do we go about applying it? First of all, you need to know just a couple of things about the average barre chord. Look at the diagram below:

You see how one of the notes isn't coloured in? That's known as the root note, and it's the note which helps to give the chord its name. The chord in the above example is a major chord; that's its type. The name of the white note tells you exactly which major chord it is. Consider this information:

C major

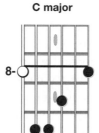

8-

This tells you that the chord is in fact a C major chord, and that it is to be played on the eighth fret. That's because the note we've been talking about is in this case a C. Move it up a fret and the chord becomes C♯ major. Same shape, different name.

It might now be occurring to you that you have twelve chords at your disposal from this one chord shape alone. Why should this be so? It sounds a bit too convenient somehow, but it's true. In order to fully grasp this labour-saving concept to its fullest extent, you will need to know what the twelve notes in music are called. (No, really, you do need to know this.) Here they are:

A A♯/B♭ B C C♯/D♭ D D♯/E♭ E F F♯/G♭ G G♯/A♭

Now, you're probably thinking "He said twelve, and if I'm not mistaken there are 17 there." That's because some notes share a name. Sorry. I didn't invent music, I'm just one of its caretakers. If we look at that series of notes again with the notes which share a name shrunk in size, things might start making better sense.

A A♯/B♭ B C C♯/D♭ D D♯/E♭ E F F♯/G♭ G G♯/A♭

Any better? The ones with the strange looking symbols after them count as one note. Just for good measure, the ♯ sign is a sharp and the ♭ is a flat and so we would see A♯ and say "A sharp". To give another example, we would see D♭ and say "D flat". Therefore, a chord symbol or name which looked like this – B♭ major – would be pronounced "B flat major". Get the idea?

Now, this is all stuff that you need to know, and for two very good reasons: firstly, you're going to have to communicate with other musicians at some point, even if it's a mate down the pub, and you don't want to find yourself pronouncing a chord like B♭ major as "B-with-a-funny-little-sign-after-it major"; secondly – and probably more importantly – these are the names of the notes on your guitar, too, and it's very wise to speak the language of music to at least this degree.

If you want to know why some notes have two names then let me tell you now that the correct attitude at this point is not to care less. Just take it at face value, be prepared for it if it comes up in magazines, books or videos, and most of all don't be intimidated by it. It's just the way that some dusty old academics decided things should be. They were probably the same people that gave perfectly ordinary garden flowers long, unpronounceable Latin names just because they could. A rose by any other name, right?

The next stage in our short-cut method of learning chords involves a little bit of writing on your part. I want you to draw a guitar neck and fill in some note names. This is a simple orienteering exercise, and one which is of significant use to you. I've produced an example below, but I would really encourage you to write out your own and take advantage of the good old-fashioned "pen memory" on offer here. Write it out reasonably large and then check it against mine. You should remember one thing, though: before you rush off to find your crayons, only

write out the "whole" notes and not the sharps and flats, OK? If you put all of the notes on, your chart will look too crowded and you won't really be able to see anything.

The finished article should look like this:

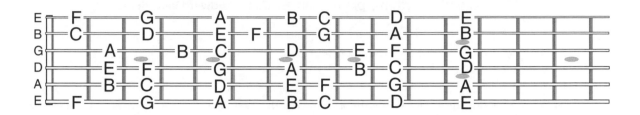

You'll soon get to understand where the sharps and flats lie on the fingerboard by using your chart. Basically, if there's a gap, there is a sharp and flat right there. However, we're not going to worry ourselves too much with them because an awful lot of guitar music uses chords of the basic letter names.

The other half of this exercise is to put your chart somewhere that you can see it when you practise. (That's also why I wanted you to write it out fairly large.) Then, every time you sit down with the guitar, give yourself simple little tests. Call out a chord type and a letter name at random – D7, for example – and find the chord on the guitar. Then call out another and do the same again. It might take you a few minutes to follow

this procedure, but I guarantee that you'll start speeding up pretty quickly if you persevere.

Don't worry either if the chord seems unclear at first or some of the notes sound muted – I'll tackle this problem later on. Sound each string one at a time, find out which notes are causing the problem and alter the pressure on your left hand until everything starts to sound right. I've got two pieces of advice here, too: remember what I said about your hand not being designed to do this and that muscles and tendons have to learn the movement – that takes time; and don't give in to the "can't do" barrier! Persevere and take on board the knowledge that thousands of guitar players have been at this exact same stage before you and have managed to see it through. You can do it, too!

PLAYING RHYTHM

"I'm more of a rhythmic player than anything." **Edward Van Halen.**

Some people say that our fundamental rhythmic sensibilities start at a very basic, organic level: the beating of our own hearts. It's a gentle, rhythmic thudding noise which accompanies every moment of our lives, beating fast and furious when we're excited, laid back and slow when we're relaxed. It's true to say that musical rhythm at least follows this basic profile: faster rhythms tend to reflect or represent excitement while slower pieces tend to sound more relaxed.

As a musician, it's important for you to know how to deal with both fast and slow music, and in order to do this you'll have to know a little bit about how rhythm works. Once again, we'll keep things simple and hopefully easy to understand.

"When it comes down to rhythm playing, it's not down to how you hold the pick or anything like that, it's where your head is at." **Nuno Bettencourt.**

Most music, if not all, has a beat. It's the thing which makes you want to tap your foot or even dance, if you're prone to exhibitionist tendencies. Knowing how to feel the beat is a fundamental part of being a guitarist. Notice the word *feel* in that last sentence. I don't mean that you merely have to understand a few basic mathematical principles or exercise the ability to recognise symbols written on a piece of paper; I mean that you have to feel music.

Even top-flight session players in orchestras would be lost without their ability to respond to some of the physical qualities within a musical performance. The whole cerebral thing of playing on the beat isn't enough. In fact, it's far from enough.

We talk about a player having a superb "feel" for music. We also talk about other related intangibles, like "the groove" or how everything is "in the pocket". This goes far beyond just making sure that everything's metrically perfect. It's much more organic than that, and it's a really difficult thing to teach.

"In a world where everyone wants to be the lead player, there's a big deficiency of rhythm playing going on. If I'm in a jam session, I'll take solos if I'm invited to, but my preference is to play rhythm, so I strongly emphasise don't just solo, get the groove going." **Bob Brozman.**

So let's look at the basics of rhythm. The ability to understand a few of its basic principles is going to be an invaluable skill to you. Oh, and I'm still not going to get too scientific, trust me.

Rhythmically speaking, music is separated into little fractions which are called *bars*. The average piece of music will be split up into bars of equal length, and each of these will form part of a song's rhythmic whole. Typically, a bar will comprise four beats, although bars of three and two beats are also pretty common. A beat is a single rhythmic cell, literally one tap of your foot. If you listen to virtually any piece of music, you should be able to hear the basic beat. Things get easier if the song concerned has drums in it because the beat is being outlined for you.

The chances are that you'll be able to hear

how the basic rhythm is being divided, too – you might be able to hear that the basic beat can be divided into groups of four. This is so because each bar has a couple of rhythmic punctuation marks, which are there to push things along. Try this experiment: put on a CD and try tapping your foot or any other convenient limb in time with the music. If you find that everything seems to be answering to a common denominator of four, try counting along. Now, there is a remote possibility that you will have stumbled on a tune which is in one of those "jazz" rhythmic signatures, which has bars comprising groups of five or seven beats. If so, nothing will fit and you'll give yourself a headache in the process. Experiment until you find something that regular folk could dance to and everything should be fine.

If you've found something "in four" and you try counting along, you'll need one more vital piece of information: where to start counting. Music isn't so organised that it always starts at the beginning of each bar, and so counting from the beginning isn't necessarily a fail-safe procedure to adopt. However, there are a couple of clues to listen out for which will aid you no end when you've got a guitar back in your hands, and so spending a little time here attempting this exercise is in no way a wasted effort.

OK, listen hard to the music. You can hear the way it's going *thud thud thud thud*, but obviously these thuds need to be organised numerically or playing with other people is going to become a nightmare. The big clue here is that the first beat of each bar is nearly always accented, and so instead of just a regular:

one two three four | one two three four |
one two three four | one two three four |

It should sound more like:

ONE two three four | ONE two three four |
ONE two three four | ONE two three four |

If you're lucky, you might find that the drummer helps you further by also accenting the third beat – not as much as beat one, but certainly more than two or four – like this:

ONE two THREE four | ONE two THREE four |

See what I mean? It may take a little while for this to become clear, and if so then don't worry, but understanding just this basic principle will help you out with both your rhythm and lead guitar playing.

So let's apply the above to guitar playing. Now that we've seen that music is divided up into metric units called bars, we'd better set about filling them with a bit of music. Before we start, though, let me just say that the following examples and general advice apply to all chord changes and not just the one I've given as an example. I've given a few simple examples so that everyone can benefit from them immediately, no matter what level they've reached. More advanced players can substitute any two chords here between which they've experienced difficulty changing. The way to overcome any glitch in changing chords is virtually the same, no matter what the chord.

If your chord-changing abilities are progressing nicely, you should have no trouble playing something like this:

| D maj / / / | D maj / / / | G maj / / / | G maj / / / | |

If you've never seen music written out like this before, it's what a *rhythm chart* looks like, and although you may come across a few variations along the way it's pretty much a universal method for writing out a chart (as they are known) for rhythm guitar.

In just the same way as before, the bars – bookended as they are here, with vertical lines – are split into four beats. However, this time we've got chord symbols and obliques (forward slashes) instead of numbers. The latter is merely shorthand for the fact that the chord is to be repeated for the whole bar – it saves a bit of writing and makes things clearer to read. I mean, which looks clearer to you? This…

| D maj D maj D maj D maj |

…or this?

| D maj / / / |

Hopefully, everyone agrees that the second one is easier on the eye. Shorter, too.

So here we have two bars of D major to play, followed by two bars of G major. Simple. However, we need to make sure that we're at least in with a winning chance of playing them in time with everyone else and getting them to sound just right, and so a few more ground rules are needed.

The word *tempo* simply means the speed at which something is being played, and we first have to agree on a tempo at which to play. Obviously there are fast tempos and slow tempos, but one man's fast is another man's "oh, that's a bit slow", and so the standard measurement here is *beats per minute* or BPM for short. A tempo of 60 BPM means that you're playing one chord per second (you can watch a clock's second hand if you're unsure here), and I think that everyone will agree that 60 is quite slow. A hundred and twenty BPM is two beats per second, and is obviously twice 60 and moderately fast. A hundred and sixty BPM is nearly three times 60, and so this is going to be fast.

Using these convenient yardsticks should be enough for now. An awful lot of music clocks in under the banner of "moderate", and so you should aim to be comfortable playing rhythm at this speed. Work up to it gradually, though – avoid struggling with any personal Everests!

Even if you think that your playing has proceeded beyond the point of simple counting and single-chord bars, it really is worth carrying out a maintenance check to make sure that your foundations are solid. I've spent many long hours curing pupils of bad habits which have been built up on dodgy foundations, and all have found it very hard to do. Returning to the basics every so often can do wonders for your playing. Even advanced guitarists need to make sure that everything is in order every so often – a sort of MOT, if you like – and just the smallest adjustment at ground level can lead to big leaps in other directions.

So now let's return to D major. For now, play these two bars using downstrokes with the plectrum – upstrokes can wait awhile. Count yourself in and try to count along as you play. It might make you feel a little silly at first, but it's a way of connecting what's going on in your head with what's going on in your hands. You're going to use this bridge between head and hands quite a lot in the future, and so it's never too early to start establishing it.

You shouldn't have any trouble playing the two bars of D major at a reasonably slow tempo, although you might find the change to G a bit of a shot in the dark to begin with. Changing chords is a hurdle we all have to get across; it's and one of the first "can't do" barriers that a lot of students encounter. A great deal of what we ask our hands to do when playing guitar is unnatural, and is certainly not what nature intended in the original design brief, so it will take you a while to persuade your body to contradict its basic design ethic so that you can change chords. The important thing here is to remember that it's got nothing to do with you being dumb, or not cut out for playing guitar; you're just fighting a couple of your body's basic design irregularities. (Of course, that's if you consider playing guitar to be a natural thing to want to do in the first place. Many parents don't...) You'll adapt to learning this new skill pretty quickly if you're patient and persistent.

If you want to check that your hands' chord-changing choreography is basically ship shape, you should follow these simple rules:

1. Chord changes happen on the beat. If you can't keep up, you're trying to play too fast. Slow down until you can play the G major chord bang on the first beat of the bar and gradually increase the tempo as you become used to the action.

2. Chord changes happen in mid-air and not on the fretboard. When you remove your fingers from the neck to change chords, the fingers should assume the new chord's shape before landing back on the fretboard and not one finger at a time. Aim for simultaneous, synchronised chord changes. If this feels awkward or impossible at first, practise it in isolation. By that I mean that you should simply sit there and swap from D major to G major a few times. You'll soon find that it starts to feel natural.

Now, a word to all of those smart alecs out there who can change between these two chords without even thinking about it. You'll definitely be confronted with an awkward chord change one day, and the method for dealing with it will still be the one outlined in the two rules stated above. The basic principle doesn't change, y'see.

Let's just check: you're playing two bars of D major and two bars of G major, using downstrokes with your pick. Everything's in time and nobody can spot the join when you change chords. Believe it or not, things don't actually get much more complicated from here on in. Much of the work in the area of changing chords is done by getting the hands and arms co-ordinated (a *physical* problem, rather than *musical*), and once nature has given in to the quirkiness of your limbs performing actions which weren't considered when the body's initial blueprints were designed things will only become easier. Well, technically speaking, at least. In fact, what will happen is that you'll find yourself having to change chords more often and over longer periods of time, but the basic work doesn't change.

In order to become good at changing chords – and by this I mean that you can readily adopt that nonchalant air of indifference to what's going on at the ends of your wrists – you'll have to practise. I don't understand why that comes as a shock to so many guitar students, but it seems to be a nasty revelation for every generation. My advice is to get hold of a songbook, magazine transcription or something similar and just work through the rhythm part methodically. Don't rush things, or create any personal Everests for yourself, or fall at the "can't do" barrier in the process. Just quiet, organised, patient practice will pay off. If you find yourself giving in to frustration at any time, just repeat the three Ps: Patience, Persistence Practice. It's the meaning of life, honestly.

Hieroglyphics

At one time in the distant past I'm sure a load of highly-qualified, academically-minded music teachers got together to make music students' lives as miserable as possible by inventing a totally idiosyncratic vocabulary for written music. Teaching it is a pain in the ass because these boys were thorough – they decided to use some Italian words (the language of the Renaissance, apparently) and mixed them up with English, a smattering of German and a couple of French words along the way. Oh, and while they were about it, why not a few Latin words, too? There's nothing like a dead language to really spice things up.

However, their real master stroke was – you're gonna love this – abbreviating them! In one or two cases, make acronyms out of them and you're guaranteed total – nay, universal – confusion. Take a look at the average piece of music and you'll see what I mean. Just remember that what you're looking at was translated from original, simple, common sense just to make music students feel miserable and you'll end up feeling a lot more cheerful. We've got to look at a few of these little gems because you'll need them in order to be able to get through a transcription, but we'll go down the "hieroglyphics lite" route, I promise you.

For a start, written music has many ways of informing you how fast a piece is to be played. To me, the most simple guide is to tell you approximately how many beats per minute you're expected to play. If you see 60 BPM then you know that a piece is quite slow, and if the marking says a speed of 160 BPM is required then you know that you'd better strap yourself in because it's going to be a fast ride.

Just to make sure that no one understands what's going on, a lot of music still has a few Italian words at the beginning which relate to tempo. You can find a full list in any music text book if you're really interested, and so I'll spare you most of the nasty details here. Just to give you some idea, though, you'll find words like *largo*, which means slow; *moderato*, which means moderate or mid tempo; and *presto*, which means fast. Most of the others are variations on these. I mean, it's vitally important that you should be provided with the information that a piece is slowish but not quite in the *largo* category, and definitely a lot more stately than *moderato*, isn't it? (Incidentally, you'll probably also come across the word *andantino*, which is one of my favourites because it means both slightly faster and slightly slower than *andante*. These guys were good, weren't they?) Most of the time, this sort of confusion won't apply to you because you'll already know a lot of the music that you're learning to play – you'll have it recorded somewhere, and so all of the potential mystery concerning its tempo will be solved beforehand. After all, it's not a crime to play something slightly slower or slightly faster, as long as everyone plays at the same speed.

The next thing you're likely to see is an indication of volume or *dynamic markings*, as they're known. Basically, this means *p*, which stands for *piano* (not the instrument; it's Italian for "soft") and which we take to mean quietly. The opposite extreme is *f*, which stands for *forte*, meaning "strong" or "loud". If something's meant to be very quiet we throw in another *p*, making it *pp*, and if we want it really loud we throw in another *f*, so *ff* means even louder. With me? I wouldn't blame you if you're not; like I said, it's really confusing and goes a long way to explaining why most musicians are basket cases.

Once again, if you already know the piece you want to play you're going to be aware of some important reference points which will be above and beyond any written version of a song you want to play, and so you'll be aware of its basic dynamics (its loud moments and its quieter passages). However, that doesn't mean that you can afford to ignore these markings. Obviously, we could apply this kind of thinking to everything and just take for granted that you don't need to be able to recognise any symbols at all, but there will be times when your memory will need a jog, and if the answer is right there before you in black and white it will probably benefit you to know how to work the system a little.

The only other important terms that I think you need to know are *DC al fine* and *DS al fine*. Both of these are shorthand symbols which tell you to repeat a section of music, as opposed to a few bars. *DC al fine* means "from the beginning to the word *fine*" (literally *da capo* [from the top] *al fine* [to the end]), and in practical terms this means that you have to play through the piece until you see the words *DC al fine*, at which point you must go back to the beginning and play until you see the word *fine*.

DS (dal segno) al fine means that you must go back to the sign (which looks like this 𝄋) and play through to the word *fine*.

In order to illustrate this more clearly, check out this chart:

fine
| one | two | three | four | five | six | seven | eight |
DC al fine

In this case, you'd play the bars in this order: one, two, three, four, five, six, seven, eight, one, two, three, four. If you saw this…

𝄋 *fine*
| one | two | three | four | five | six | seven | eight |
DS al fine

…you'd play the bars in this order: one, two, three, four, five, six, seven, eight, three, four.

If none of this makes any sense, don't worry – you'll pick it all up through the simple act of playing songs. Remember my point about the "pathfinder" generation of guitar players, who learned their craft by playing along with records and getting into bands as soon as possible. If you apply a similar reasoning today, there's no reason for the magic to fail this time around.

> "Your hand is always moving – it's always somehow rhythmically involved. You gotta be sort of like a drummer inside yourself."
> **Nuno Bettencourt.**

Another mistake that a lot of guitar players make is that they take everything that they see as if it were carved in stone. Remember, music is basically an art form and therefore repels all attempts to systematise it with a rigorous, unchangeable set of rules. If people didn't challenge the system occasionally we wouldn't have had Jimi Hendrix or Eric Clapton. Guitar playing tends to evolve in fits and starts. At the time of writing this book, I have absolutely no idea where it's heading next – only time will tell. However, I know that it will turn around again, and that someone will square the circle and come up with something totally unexpected.

If we think of bending a few simple rules and not taking everything at face value with chords, then just because a chord symbol like this crops up…

A maj

…it doesn't mean that it has to played in the conventional way, as a strum from the fifth string to the first. This is the downside to simple chordal notation: it's sometimes a little too open to interpretation. If you've learned that A major is a chord shape which looks like this…

…then you could be a little bit nervous about playing it any other way, just in case it's wrong or inappropriate. In fact, there are a great many ways

of interpreting any single chord, and a lot of the time it's up to you to decide exactly how. (This is, of course, unless you are playing something "as written" from a song you've heard on CD and you want to play as close to the original as possible. Even in this case, you still might be met with some very ambiguous chord symbols.)

"Usually, when people start to use chords they start getting into these beautiful-sounding notes, and they try to make the biggest-sounding E chords and stuff like that; but eventually you find yourself going the other way and saying 'How can I get the same information by using the smallest amount of notes?'" **Joe Satriani.**

Shape Shifting

I'm not going to go into too much detail here, but I will say that it's probably as well to prepare yourself for playing abbreviated chords quite often as an accompanist. For instance, if we take just this one chord symbol of A major, it's possible to play it in a number of different ways. The important thing is to both see and hear it as A. Here are a few examples:

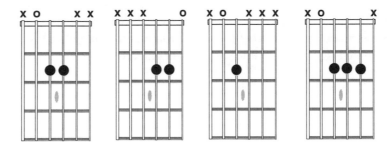

If we were to interpret A major as a barre chord, a few more abbreviations come into the frame:

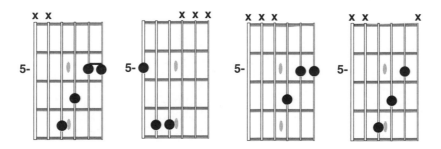

You can extend this so that it applies to the five basic ways in which you can play the chord of A major ascending up the fretboard, where you would have these shapes available to you:

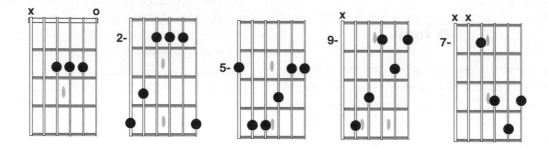

Then, when you understand that it's possible to play only two or three notes within the chord shape each time and still land dead on the money, you will begin to realise that a chord symbol can be interpreted in literally a dozen different ways.

> "You can take any one of our songs and move them up and play them as barre chords and they're just not the same songs any more. They've lost width and depth somehow." **Malcolm Young.**

Option Anxiety

Before you start getting worried about which chord shape to use, let me assure you that this kind of chordal knowledge takes time to accumulate. The best ways of storing up this knowledge are to play with other people, to work through transcriptions (keeping an eye on what you're being asked to play – it's probably something familiar, even it doesn't look it) and to watch other players. Some versions of chords sound better than others in certain situations, and only by gaining experience will you obtain the necessary information on which to base your choice.

Once you've made up your mind that you're OK about things taking their time, and that you're not tempted to rush things, then you'll find that your chord database grows naturally. It's not a party trick. It's not a case of being able to say: "Look how many shapes I know for single chord!" You merely remember the ones that sound good in different contexts.

LEAD

"The main thing I was doing was not playing guitar style clichés; not so much rock but blues guitar clichés. That was something that was a mission!" **Steve Howe.**

It might be wise for me to start off by defining what I mean by lead guitar. This is the area of guitar playing that is confined to playing the melody, guitar solos or whatever you'd like to call them. Despite the fact that this might take up a huge fraction of a guitarist's time when he's practising, it actually only constitutes about ten per cent of the average performance. The emphasis here, I've always believed, is in the wrong place. For a start, a lot of the time you end up practising the wrong things.

The elements of rhythm that we've been examining also apply playing lead guitar to a significant degree and should not be ignored, and so everything that you've learned from the section on rhythm guitar can be applied to and included in your lead playing.

I suppose it's a fact that the rhythm player in a band can be hidden in amongst the other aspects of the song's accompaniment. He can sit back with the bass player, keyboard player, drummer etc and remain fairly inconspicuous. However, this is not the case for the lead player. Yet despite this, I still believe that in many cases the balance between practising lead and rhythm is all wrong, and a lot of lead guitarists ignore some of the more vital aspects of their craft. For instance, we will see how rhythm is important for a lead player in terms of phrasing, and yet any practice in this vital area is often abandoned in favour of learning another solo or fraternising with scales.

When people ask me what I think is the most important attribute that a lead guitarist should have, they expect me to say "Why, his knowledge of the fretboard and scales, of course," but I don't. I think a sense of melody is far more important than anything else because a lead player is really just playing a melody. You can define it as a guitar solo or whatever else you'd like to call it, but really, when it comes down to it, it's a melody. The jazz guitarist Martin Taylor said that he was introduced to the concept of soloing for jazz guitar by being told by his father that all he would be doing would be offering an alternative melody to that of the song, and I think that that is an aspect which is forgotten by an awful lot of lead guitar players.

You can always tell good players from bad ones. A poorly-developed player tends to play a solo that has absolutely no respect for what has gone before in the song. It just doesn't fit. It's a little vignette – complete in itself, perhaps, but it has no relation to what has gone before or what will follow it. The most successful guitar solo, in my opinion, is one which fits into a song as if it were a part of the song's main body, literally hanging onto the melody and everything that's gone before.

The great jazz guitar player Joe Pass said that a lot of jazz guitar students forget the fact that they're meant to be playing within the character of the piece. It might come as no surprise that these guitar players haven't actually learned the melody of the original song to which they are adding a solo. Joe even suggested that a guitarist should pay an awful lot of attention to the lyrical content of a song as well – after all, you don't want to provide a solo which is far removed from the character of the song's lyrical content. It's no good producing a happy, major-key-sounding solo in a song which is about a basically very sad topic – a blues, for instance. There are plenty of examples of inappropriate solos that have been recorded in the past, but I'm too much the gentleman to start naming names. You can probably think of a few yourself. Basically, if it sounds wrong, it is wrong! That's a thing that you should repeat to yourself. In fact, it might be a good idea to write it down somewhere and keep it within view every time you practise. I personally reject the notion that a lead guitarist is nothing but a rhythm guitarist who's done a little more practice. This just isn't the case.

The roles of lead and rhythm guitarists can be strictly defined. They can perhaps be typified as the roles that Malcolm and Angus Young perform in the band AC/DC. Malcolm certainly doesn't tread on Angus' toes, and yet Angus finds himself playing rhythm a lot of the time, even though he is without doubt the lead guitarist. To be a successful lead guitarist you have to be a bit of an all-rounder. Everybody wants to play solos, and few people aspire to being a rhythm guitarist, even though there are some great examples of very, very fine rhythm guitar players in rock and pop.

So let's get on with having a look at how we can turn you into a fine lead guitar player. To do this, just as before we're going to look at the separate roles performed by the right and left hands, kicking off with the good old right hand.

THE RIGHT HAND

"Hank Marvin had a Strat and it was all I ever wanted." **David Gilmour.**

In the first section of this book we looked at the right hand's role in rhythm playing, and we considered the angle of the pick, the gauge of the string and even the gauge of the pick itself. None of these are set to change. Obviously, if you've settled on something that works for rhythm playing we're not going to mess around with it for your lead style; we merely adapt what we've already got.

One of the main differences is that you'll be playing more single notes when playing lead. This implies that your picking technique is going to have to be examined, and is going to have to be refined. So far you might have confined yourself to playing chords, and maybe the odd single note, but now you're definitely going to have to focus on the right hand even more.

A lead player's picking hand is going to be slightly more athletic than a rhythm player's. This doesn't mean that it has to be any better (some of the finest rhythm parts on records are quite awkward to play), but it does mean that you're going to have certain duties to perform that you may not have discovered when you were exploring your rhythm technique.

At this point it's worth looking at the section we touched on briefly in the first section of the book, which is the angle at which the pick presents itself to the strings. I will say again that you should aim to have a slightly "edge-on" pick attack, so that the left-hand side of the pick hits the strings first and the hand sweeping across the strings describes a very natural arc. If you like, you can explore for yourself the difference in sound which the various picking angles give you. Fret any note with the left hand and try angling the pick differently while picking

constantly. You should be able to hear a significant difference. You may not even agree that the sound produced when the left-hand side of the pick hits the string first is the best, and of course you must follow your own inclinations. As I've said already, I can only pass on knowledge from the mainstream of music performance; the minute we become too eclectic we're in trouble.

Lead Picking

To start with, it might be a good idea to spend a little bit of idle time just picking each individual string, from the bass string over to the top treble string – from E to E, in other words. Just pick each string individually. This will give the hand a good idea where each individual string lies under its span. You're giving it another set of those all-important reference points we looked at in the rhythm section. These reference points now have to be refined; after all, we're dealing with individual strings and not groups or sets of strings.

Make sure that you use both up and down strokes alternately. This is known as *alternate picking*, and is a staple exercise in learning how to pick cleanly and efficiently. If you haven't come across this picking convention already, programme it into your fingers now because it is a method for picking which will lead you towards reaching the correct platform from which you'll be able to pick virtually anything in the future.

If you sit there for a while, idly picking each string on the guitar one at a time, this will start the process off nicely. A by-product, of course, is that it will drive everybody in the room with you stark raving mad, so it might be good to fiddle around somewhere that you'll upset the least number of people possible. In all seriousness, I believe that guitar practice ought to be done away from people, away from the family and certainly away from the television set. Too many guitarists have adopted a practice routine in which they sit slumped in front of the television, idly looking at the screen and not concentrating on what they're doing with either hand. This is no good. You can play like that if you want, but I put an emphasis on the word *play* here and not *practise*. Practice is a serious business, and you'll find that you can minimise the amount of practice that you need to do and still progress quite quickly as long as you adhere to certain rules. A couple of hours slouched in front of a soap opera on the TV isn't going to produce much in the way of results (except in that of the alienation of your loved ones, of course), but ten minutes a day of concentrated practice in controlled surroundings will guarantee that your playing progresses.

In any case, as you play this one-note-a-time exercise across your guitar, you might as well remember the rules. Basically, the picking hand has to remain relaxed. That old enemy tension can't enter the scene here at all. You must strive to rid the hand of it, and believe me a few minutes a day spent taking good care of your picking hand will mean that you will progress an awful lot faster in the long run.

It's very easy to practise things badly. I've spent many hours with pupils correcting their past mistakes as far as picking is concerned, and they've found it very, very difficult to get out of habits that have been long formed. What we're looking to do here is trying and learn some good habits, habits that will form a very strong foundation in your playing and will stay with you for the rest of your musical life, so please be sure that there is no tension whatsoever present in your right hand. If you can detect it, try and remove it. Just remember that the golden word here is *relax*. If you can avoid tension then you'll stay out of trouble in terms of bad technique, and you'll also avoid the medical complaints that tend to accompany repetitive movement in this way.

Anchorage

We looked earlier at the question of anchoring your hand. Here it's no different. However, whereas following some rhythm techniques meant that you weren't anchoring your hand at all (that is to say that the hand had to be totally free), for lead playing in general there has to be some sort of reference point, and so once again I would recommend that the fingertips of the hand should occasionally dust the top of the guitar's scratch plate underneath the top E string. It's like touching the edge of the swimming baths – early learners need know that it's there all the time.

In this way you will avoid a dreadful habit from which every guitarist on MTV seems to suffer, who seem to look at their hands far more than should be necessary. In my opinion, there's no reason for this at all. In fact, while you're playing guitar – from the audience's point of view – the last place you want to look is at your hands. Remember that you're out there performing, you're not standing there like a very introvert statue which is no fun to look at at all. When you're on the stage, with lights dazzling your eyes, you can't see any more than six yards in front of you, but even so you might as well look around.

If you find that you need the odd visual check on the fretboard – and we all do from time to time – then this is fine, but in general it's better to learn to avoid staring fixedly at either hand. One positive aspect of learning to play classical guitar is that students are taught to look at the music they're playing from the word go, and in this way they automatically learn not to look at their hands. It can be done; it just takes a little discipline.

Scales

At the beginning of this book I said that I was going to take you through the fundamentals of guitar playing without labouring you with long, boring names, and I'm going to keep that promise. However, there are advantages to actually familiarising yourself with a few shapes on the guitar.

I'm personally very perplexed about the way in which scales and modes have overtaken the guitarist's vocabulary in the last 20 years, and it's very possible that guitar magazines are at fault here. We have tended to centre in on the area of technique to such an extent that a great many guitar students have gained the impression that technique is the most important thing in playing guitar, and that, along with technique, the naming of objects and the naming of scales is of equal and vital importance. The result of this is that we now have a generation of guitarists who are very literate in terms of tablature, to the extent that their musical ears and their ability to hear music has suffered as a result. They can also play scales at lightning speed against a metronome, but no music evolves from their practising at all.

I don't want to sound like an old trooper and start every sentence with "In my day…" but I will say that, in the early days, most of my generation of guitar players learned by slowing down records and listening to phrases over and over again until we could work them out on our guitars. Before my generation, of course, there were the jazz and blues guitarists of the Thirties and Forties. I once had the pleasure of spending an evening with the great jazz legend Tal Farlow, and he told me that the reason why he thought that he had developed such a fine musical ear and could play most of the music that he heard in his head – or, for that matter, anywhere else – was because he learned guitar by listening to the radio. In this way, he told me, you've only got one chance – you can't repeat things or slow them down; you have to get it right the first time or else you don't get it at all. I heard a similar story when I talked to blues legend Buddy Guy.

A by-product of learning guitar in this way is that both of these players – and many more like them – developed a set of musical reflexes that would aid them greatly in their future careers. They couldn't have told you the names of the scales they were learning (most of the time they were learning melodies, not stale scale exercises, anyway), but all of the knowledge filtered through to their musical cores. The rest is history.

These days, guitarists have it all handed to them on a plate. Most of the great solos of all time have been transcribed somewhere and are available in tablature, a series of numbers which are about as musical as the telephone book. Having learned in this way, a good percentage of players haven't developed an innate sense of music. So what we are going to try to do here is develop your ears so that you know things are *right*, and in order to bring this about I'm going to go completely against everything you may have read on this subject before because I'm going to keep the use of names to an absolute minimum. Instead, I'll just give you a few ideas and shapes of sounds on the instrument. It's up to you to work with this material and try to turn it into music. I'm not going to write out solos for you; later in the book I'll be showing you how to put a solo together from nothing at all. What I'm going to do is try and teach you how to develop your ear so that the rest will follow.

We're also going to be looking at how to learn solos from records, a practice that I wish I could single-handedly re-introduce to the guitar-playing populace. It's a skill that has sadly fallen into abandon, and I think that an awful lot of musical damage has been suffered because of this. Maybe we can put things right.

If properly schooled, your ear will become your best ally on the instrument. It can help you store up all sorts of information, and will help you to build up your musical reflexes. Joe Pass wrote a chord book which is singularly one of the most useful chord books that I think I've ever seen, although there's one quirk about it which you don't see in any other chord book: he doesn't name any of the chords. Now, you might be thinking "What use is that?" In fact, I actually had a pupil come to me on one occasion with Joe's chord book under his arm, imploring me to write the names of the chords underneath the diagrams so that he could learn their names. Of course, I started off by doing exactly what he wanted, but then all of a sudden the penny dropped and I got the point. Joe didn't want to name the chords because he didn't want you to know the names; he wanted the student to know them by sound. For a long time, Joe Satriani used the Pass chord book as a kind of mantra.

"When I was developing my chord vocabulary, I happened upon a book by Joe Pass called *Joe Pass: Chords* containing what looked to me like chord fragments. They were listed by chord groups and not by individual names… There was every C6, Cmaj13, Cmaj9, C6/9 etc that you could think of, and his idea was to memorise all that, and then the next time a song called for a C chord you made your mind up based on your feelings about the music rather than following the direction of some chord chart. So…every night after dinner I would just play every one of those chords, and after a while your fingers get very limber, and if you're doing around 300 chords in about 20 minutes, every night, you begin to remember them!

"When I started, I couldn't imagine the brain power necessary to memorise 300 chords, but I knew that, if I just kept on doing it, I would become a natural, and maybe I wouldn't have to work so hard. It worked because at that time I was doing a lot of jamming with my friends, and I remember one night we were doing some pseudo-jazz piece and I suddenly thought "Oh right, minor seven". Everyone was strumming a minor seven chord and I did something…and they all looked at me and said "Whoah, what was that?" I was just doing what Joe Pass had intended, which was just a kind of leap of faith to do what you think, it might work – and it did!" **Joe Satriani.**

Remarkable isn't it? Now, you might not think that this sort of thing is possible; you might think that this enters the realm of science fiction. I mean, to get musical ears like that…well, you have to be born with them, don't you? I don't believe this to be the case. I believe that, if your interest in music is such that you have this insatiable curiosity to discover more and more things about the instrument, you can develop a musical ear. Anybody can.

I wouldn't say that my own musical ear was the best in its field by any means. I know plenty of people who can actually blow me off the planet in terms of being able to a fix a pitch just by ear; some of the guys who work for *Guitar Techniques* have such incredible powers as far as musical recognition is concerned that they leave me with my jaw firmly on the floor. My point is that I've developed an average-to-good musical ear which has certainly not held me back and has got me pretty much everywhere I've wanted to go.

Developing a musical ear is really a leap of faith, and it's a leap of faith I'm going to ask you to take in this book. We're going to be looking at a few chord names, and we're also going to be looking at a few musical conventions, such as keys and things like that, because I think that these are essential. After all, it's no good turning up at a jam session in a pub and being told that you're expected to play a solo on a blues in G without knowing what G is. It's possible to take things like that for granted. I think that everyone will agree with me that you need to know the fundamentals at least, and don't worry – there are some easy ways of getting your head around this sort of thing. Just bear with me.

How Many Scales?

It's a sad fact that people have lost touch with the idea that most music is made up of fairly commonplace elements. It might come as a shock to you that an awful lot of music is made up of the simplest of scales and the simplest of chords, and I believe that our learning should reflect this. If at any point in your learning you feel it necessary to venture into music's more dark and dusky corners then fair enough, go for it; but I'm telling you now, with my hand on my heart, that most music can be accessed by very, very fundamental means. You don't need to learn a phrygian dominant scale before you have fully come to terms with scales which are in far more common use. This is another mistake that I believe is made by an awful lot of guitar students, who try to run before they can walk. It's important to build up a vocabulary of the fundamentals before you look at anything exotic, and so we're only going to look at a couple of scales. The one with which I want to start is the guitarist's most favourite scale of all.

Although this scale has a name, this is a fact that we've agreed is secondary in terms of its importance in music. It's called a pentatonic scale, in which *pente* is a Greek word meaning "five" and "tonic" stems from another Greek word, *tonos*, which means "tone". In other words, it's a five-note scale.

There are pentatonic scales in virtually every culture on the planet, and most of them are very, very old. I'm told that the earliest form of pentatonic scale was actually prevalent in Egypt, in thousands of years BC, and so we are talking extremely ancient culture here.

There are all sorts of reasons why five-note scales entered every musical culture across the world, and I shan't bore you with them here. If you're at all interested in musicology, there are libraries full of books on the subject which will give you fairly rational explanations why pentatonic scales came into being. I have my own beliefs on the subject, but let's drop the topic there, shall we?

The pentatonic – or five-note – scale is one which you can use maybe as much as 90% of the time on the guitar and still put on a fairly good show of playing some excellent guitar solos. This might come as a bit of a startling fact but it's absolutely true. It's that fundamental.

You shouldn't confuse it with the blues scale, but I'll forgive you if you do. The difference between the pentatonic scale and the blues scale is so negligible that they could easily be mistaken for one another, and we're not really going to bother with exact definitions here. My advice is to become familiar with the shapes of pentatonic scales on the guitar fretboard. Believe me, it's going to help you in the long run.

At both guitar seminars and in private tuition I often meet students who swear blind that they know the pentatonic scale, but I find otherwise after only a very few minutes. They've learned maybe only one shape for it. There are actually five pentatonic scales, and learning five shapes isn't too much different from just learning one. Well, it's certainly not five times as difficult.

I believe that it's necessary to learn all five of these shapes, and I implore you to do so. At a recent seminar I encountered a pupil who had nominated himself for the advanced class and yet confessed that he didn't know the five basic pentatonic shapes. This is a bit of a strange definition of "advanced" in my book.

So there's a little bit of learning to do here, but we're going to learn the pentatonic scale slightly differently to the way in which convention dictates. Sure, you've got to learn to play it, and you've got to learn to pick it, and you've got to learn to make it sound good, and we'll come to that a bit later; but for now I want you to learn to sing it. It might sound a little daft to start with, and certainly if you attempt this in public or amongst family members they'll probably try to have you certified within a very short time, so once again I would recommend that practice time is probably best spent away from the family and, well, society in general. It doesn't matter if you can't sing in tune; I want to get the notes of this scale inside your head, because that's the place where guitar solos are born.

Let's deal with this here and now. When a singer sings into a microphone, what's the most important thing that's going on? Is it the type of microphone? The lead which connects the microphone to a PA? The type of PA? The speaker enclosures? Maybe the fact that the mixer has applied compression, reverb or echo? No, none of these are important because if you took all of that away you'd still be left with a singer who could either sing or not. When a singer sings a note, the note doesn't start just before the microphone; it starts deep within him.

It's easier to think in this way because, of course, you're thinking "Well, of course it does – it starts in his lungs. He's got to breathe, dammit!" However, by this I mean that he has to fix the pitch somehow. So how is this done? It's by a relationship between the brain and the vocal cords that the note is formed. Have you noticed how some singers can pitch notes perfectly on their first attempts? They don't have to practise them, or waver around a pitch (or, if they do, they're not going to hold down a job for very long). The note comes out perfect, pure and clean from the start.

Just because you've got a guitar in your hands, this doesn't mean that you can do things any differently. That note has to be within you, even though you're using fingertips, wire, wood and electromagnetics to produce your note not rather than your vocal cords. Even so, all of this is irrelevant; the place where music starts is inside you.

Another popular misconception shared by many guitar students is that a guitarist is thinking about scales when he's playing. There's a wealth of evidence to the contrary.

Music Spoken Here

Few guitar students believe that they will ever be capable of this kind of musical thinking, but wait a second – is it that different from learning a language and then being able to think in that language? This is something that we've all done already, and can do without any effort at all.

Furthermore, when we talk, we are mainly improvising; we're certainly not reading a script, or thinking about the fundamentals of grammar and checking to make sure that our sentences contain verbs. We don't plan what we say sentences ahead; we've got a general idea of what we're going to be saying, and we talk around a point or theme.

This isn't so very different from playing guitar and knowing what you're going to play. You've got a series of notes in your head, you've got some idea of the theme you're meant to be playing, and

you just go for it. There's no consciousness attached to it, specifically. People may not believe that they can improvise, and yet every time they answer a question they're improvising. Musical improvisation is exactly the same.

This is where humming what you're learning is vitally important. It's a matter of getting those notes inside your head (in much the same way that you learned English) and abandoning the idea that you're going to be playing random notes and then trying to make sense of them as you play them. Musical phrases happen first inside the head before they're allowed to flow out onto the guitar.

One player summed up how improvisation works very eloquently, saying that it's just like humming in the shower, or singing with your fingertips. Basically, improvisation is nothing more than this, but somehow those notes have to start off inside you and not on the fretboard. So do me a favour and try humming these notes as you learn them, because after a while you'll forget all about shapes, you'll forget about keys, you'll forget about names and things like that, and you'll just be able to play.

There's a famous quote from the great jazz saxophone player Charlie Parker, who said: "Learn all your scales. Then forget that shit and just play." I think that we can apply that here.

THE LEFT HAND

"I wrote 'Show Me The Way' in the morning and 'Baby I Love Your Way' just as the sun was setting the same day. I'm still trying to work out what I had for breakfast." **Peter Frampton.**

Let's start off this section of the book by exploding another misconception held by many guitar students, which would have you believe that it is the gear that you use – your guitar, amp, etc – that has the primary influence over your overall tone as a guitarist. I guess that I believed it myself for a number of years, back when I was wondering why my Les Paul copy didn't make me sound like Eric Clapton. Surely if I had a real one and a Marshall stack the job would be done for me? Oops. Well, I was only a kid, and there was no one around to tell me any differently. The electric guitar was still considered disreputable, and music as a profession was a definite no-no, so there weren't books or magazines or teachers around to put me straight. The only guitar tuition available to me was classical or folk, so gimme a break, OK?

Nevertheless, this is a fault that I have seen in many players, even today, despite the fact that now magazines, books and teachers all yell "Untrue!" from every direction.

The fact is that your sound, tone, touch, feel, sonic thumbprint, or whatever you want to call it, is as personal to you as your signature. It's all wrapped up in your personality, and don't let any box of tricks in a guitar shop window convince you of anything else. The biggest influence on the way you sound as a guitar player is, quite simply, the way in which you touch the strings and the quirky personal nuances you introduce to your basic right- and left-hand technique. Add to this your own sense of melody or choice of notes, chord voicing preferences and so on, and you have the beginnings of style.

> "I would say that your style does not appear overnight. You need to find it; you need to nurture it." **Carl Verheyen.**

If you're still after proof that the shiny new guitar in the store window won't make you sound too different to the way you do now, I'll offer a few examples.

Case Histories

I was interviewing Steve Vai (one of the more pleasurable aspects of my day job, I might mention), and I was aware that he wouldn't have a guitar with him, and so as I intended the interview to cover some aspects of technique I took one of my own along. It was an old Charvel guitar, which I'd used for countless gigs and with which I was quite happy, but at the same time it was nothing special, just a generic "superstrat".

However, we got to the point in the interview at which Steve was trying to tell me about a technique he had discovered which added a quirky edge to harmonics. In order to get the point across, he said "Here, give me your guitar," and I handed over the Charvel. He played a few notes on it, and my guitar instantly sounded like Steve Vai, something that I hadn't been able to make it do. He handed it back to me, and the next time I picked it up it sounded just like me again.

As a footnote to this story, I must add that the guitar wasn't actually plugged in during the interview. Steve's influence over my guitar's sound was purely acoustic. It was his touch which worked the magic, and that alone.

On another occasion I was to interview Joe Satriani (look, it's a tough job but somebody has to edit a guitar magazine), and once again there was the distinct possibility that Joe wouldn't have a guitar with him. This time I happened to have an Ibanez JS guitar to hand, and so I took it along to the interview. As it turned out, Joe had one of his JS Silver Surfer guitars with him, but he took a fancy to the one I'd brought along because it was a black one, and he said that it would look good in the pictures we were taking to accompany the feature. A few photographs were taken of Joe with the black one and a few of him holding the silver one, and he swapped from one to the other while I held the one that wasn't currently in use. Now, we know that guitarists are born fidgets with guitars, and so I couldn't resist having a quick go on the silver guitar while Joe gave the black one a good seeing to for the camera. You know, it was uncanny; Joe played the black one and it sounded like him, but when he gave it back to me it sounded like me. The same thing happened with the silver guitar. Once again, nothing was plugged in.

Recently, I attended a soundcheck at a venue at which Brian May was playing. Now, if there's one person in rock guitar who has an immediately recognisable sound it's Brian – I think that we'd all agree on that one. Despite the fact that Brian has a rather unique set-up in terms of amplification, and a very specific home-made guitar, when his tech was testing the rig to make sure that everything worked it sounded like a good rock guitar, nothing more. However, the minute Brian took the guitar and strummed a first position A major chord it was an instant transition to the beginning of the guitar in Queen's 'We Will Rock You'. It simply couldn't have been anyone else, but it certainly had nothing to do with the guitar or the amp set-up; there was something going on that was far less concerned with hardware.

Case proven? I hope so, because abandoning this illusion will save you a fortune, as well as a lot of heartache.

Left Field

It's my belief that the left hand has a very large part to play in creating a good sound on an electric (or, for that matter, an acoustic) guitar. It's the hand that actually touches the strings, pressing them to the wood of the fingerboard and carrying out certain techniques which all

combine to form any note's or chord's sonic characteristic. For your convenience, I've grouped these techniques together into a teachable format, and they give us these main areas to cover:

Vibrato
Bending
Sliding
Hammers
Pulls

So let's look at them one at a time.

Vibrato

I'll start by talking about vibrato because it's without doubt the most important characteristic that your left hand has to learn. If you want a dictionary definition, vibrato is the act of moving the string from side to side when you play, which enhances the string's movement and adds resonance. Sounds grand, doesn't it? To return to basics, it's really just the way in which you wiggle the strings with the fingers on your left hand to make them growl or sing a bit more.

I'm using the word "sing" here quite intentionally because it's almost beyond doubt that this is why we add vibrato to a note, to imitate natural vibrato in a voice. Nearly every instrument uses it to some degree, with a few notable exceptions, such as the piano, unless I'm missing something here. Wind instruments like trumpet, saxophone and so on have the advantage of being breath powered, and so have a natural vocal personality to them. (Some cynics would say that it's the only personality that sax players have.) However, we string players have to add it artificially, and we're not alone in this; our brethren who play violin, cello and double bass, etc, all have to learn how to do it, too (although it has to be said that classical vibrato is somewhat less extreme than its rock 'n' roll counterpart). I've provided a set of audio reference points on the accompanying CD for all of this, but we'll also need to look at the basics on paper.

To begin with, play the third string at the seventh fret, as shown here.

Third finger

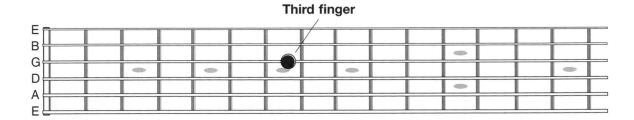

Play the note with your third finger, laying your first and second fingers on the same string behind your third in order to give you some support. Don't grip the neck – no tension should be present in your hand. If there is, it will stop you from moving your hand freely.

Next, move the string from side to side. That is, adopt a combined movement of pulling the string slightly towards the floor and slightly towards the ceiling. Don't move your hand from left to right – that's classical guitar vibrato, and it won't be effective enough here.

Start slowly on this one; you can concentrate on building up your speed later on. Vibrato happens at different speeds, but you'll still be using practically everything that you learn here. The exact distance that you make the string travel in each direction is something best left to the ears rather than the eyes. I'm not going to give you precise measurements because I don't know them myself. You'll know when your vibrato technique is right because it will start to sound right. Work with the audio examples on the CD and you shouldn't go too far wrong.

I would advise you to practise this technique without an amplifier at first. In fact, this advice is good for most techniques. An amp can deceive you into thinking that your vibrato technique is better and more solid than it is. If you practise acoustically, what you're hearing is the sound of your fingers on the strings before any artificial colouring has been applied later on in the signal path. I don't practise with an amp at all. One reason for this is that I live in a flat, and I'm very conscious that my neighbours probably aren't as enchanted with the sound of electric guitar as I am. Another reason is that I want to hear what I can do with my fingers before I plug in and let other people hear it, too. In this way I figure that I'm asking less from

the amplifier because I've tried to wring as much tone out of my guitar at source.

Vibrato comes from the wrist and forearm in a combined movement that's not unlike turning a door handle, so take a while to watch out for this movement and make sure that there is no tension present at any time.

Once you have your vibrato on the rails, feel free to start speeding it up slowly and practising it on all strings in all fret positions. As an additional exercise, I would advise you to listen to a few of your favourite guitarists play, paying special attention to their vibrato. You should know what you're listening for from your own endeavours in the field. This isn't a skill that will come too quickly, although I have taught pupils who have got it immediately. However, if you apply the three Ps and avoid personal Everests, you should be OK.

String Bending

This is another technique which causes a great deal of unnecessary distress for guitar students – usually, it has to be said, because they never practise bending in any specific, focused way. Remember: if you have any weak spots at all, by learning to recognise them, categorising them as either musical or physical, isolating them and spending a little time each day practising them, you'll find that you can deal with them. There aren't too many occasions on which you can say this but *this procedure always works*.

String bending is another very important technique to master. All rock and pop styles employ it, although jazz players tend to use it the least, largely due to the heavy-gauge strings they use and the stylistic foundations of the genre. On the other hand, nearly all rock and pop players use bending as an intrinsic part of their overall style of playing.

▼ **TRACK 16**

If you think about it, the very act of bending a string – pushing against about 16lb of pressure – requires physical development, and this certainly puts bending under the *physical* section of our diagnostic chart. However, knowing when to bend, how far to bend and, more importantly, when to stop bending is very much on the *musical* side. Your ear will determine when you've reached the correct pitch but your fingers will need to be strong enough to apply the subtle, controlled pressure necessary to get the string where it needs to be.

The exercise I give people to ascertain if their picking is making it or not couldn't be simpler: first, fret the note at the seventh fret on the G string in exactly the same way as you did before (that is, using your third finger with the other two

laying behind it on the same string for added support). Next, sound the top E string and, while it's still ringing, bend the note, pushing with all three of your fingers, until the two notes agree. This is what I meant about string bending being both a musical and a physical task.

To begin with, that's all you have to do. Get the two notes to agree, repeat the exercise a few times, and then move on to something else. When you're absolutely sure that you can play it right every time, try experimenting a little. Pick any note on the top three strings and then try to bend up to the pitch of that note from a position two frets behind it. For example, if you choose the note at the tenth fret on the B string, try to bend up to its pitch from the eighth fret, like this:

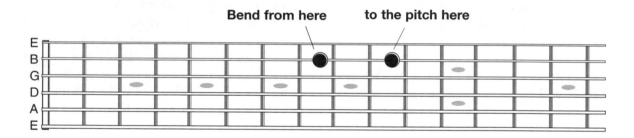

You can develop this exercise by bending notes anywhere on the fretboard. The rule always stays the same, however: play a note and bend the string to the higher pitch. Always give yourself the opportunity to hear the note you're trying to reach beforehand, as this will do your ear a lot of good.

Sometimes I'm asked what notes are best for bending in any particular scale, and the only answer I can give is "Try them all and see which ones you like." It all becomes a part of your style,

and that, as we've seen, is a very personal thing.

Sliding

This is another technique which is generally overlooked in many people's practice plan. Sliding is the practice by which a guitarist changes position on the neck of the instrument. If you've been looking at scale diagrams, the chances are that you will have noticed that they tend to take place straight across the neck of the guitar, from the string nearest you to the one that's farthest away.

TRACK 17

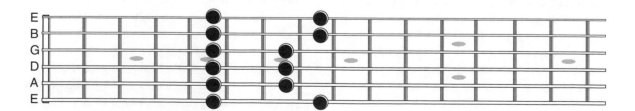

The scale above stays in one position, which means that you don't actually have to move your hand to the left or right along the fretboard in order to play it. This is all very well and good, but what happens if you want to play something like this?

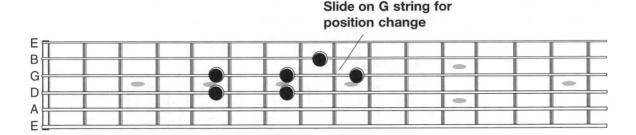

Slide on G string for position change

In this case you have to move your left hand up the string and shift position. You make this move by sliding, and the sound of the slide itself has well and truly entered the guitar's vocabulary.

When a player first tries this technique it's like driving a car with faulty brakes: you're not sure where you're going to stop. Once again, practice will sort out this problem for you, if you apply the three Ps.

To begin with, all that you have to do in order to practise the technique of sliding is to pick two notes that are fairly close together on the same string and slide between them. In the same way as we did with bending, play the destination pitch first and then slide towards it. Your ear should tell you when to stop sliding.

If you want something more involved with which to practise your sliding, look at the two examples below:

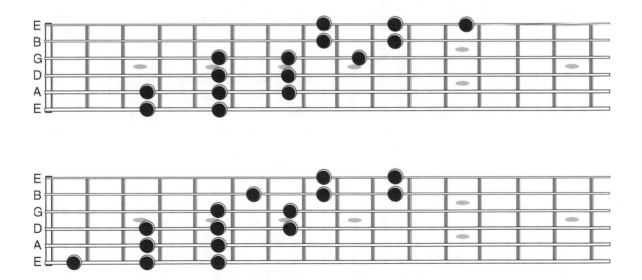

These are pentatonic scales (more about these later), and they flow across the neck diagonally, so playing them calls for a great deal of sliding. The fingering remains the same throughout the exercise, however; you're using only fingers one and three on your left hand. By playing through these two scales as part of your daily practice plan you'll be doing your ears a lot of good, while at the same time you'll also be sorting out the more physical aspects of learning to slide. There are some audio slide examples on the CD, so you can hear what they sound like in the field.

Hammers

You might have heard this particular technique referred to as "hammer-ons". I personally prefer the term "hammers", but it's the same technique. Hammering is the practice by which you pluck the guitar string once with the pick and then actually play two or more notes above the one you've just played. This technique calls for a certain degree of physical development, as you'll see.

In order to play a hammer, play the note at the fifth fret on the G string with the first finger, like this:

First finger

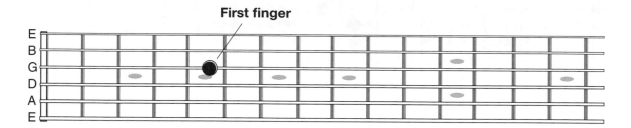

Now, while the note is still ringing, lower your third finger onto the same string at the seventh fret.

Keep first finger down   **Hammer with third finger**

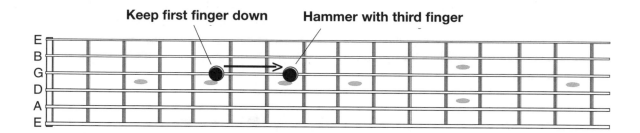

You should hear two notes from the one pick stroke, and what's more they should be at the same approximate volume. This is how you can tell if you're doing it right: the two notes should be at the same volume. This means that your third finger must hit the string with enough force to make the note ring without the added help of a pick stroke. You can experiment with the level of weight you have to employ – you'll know when you've got it right.

This is an exercise that you can do all over the guitar neck. Just place your hand down anywhere, on any string, play a note with your first finger and hammer down the third, making sure that the two notes are of equal volume. Simple.

Extending this technique, you can then work up to playing a note with the first finger and then hammering down the remaining three fingers on the left hand and seeing if you get four in a row,

although I would advise against trying this too soon. Remember that muscles are developing here as well as reflexes, and you don't want to suffer from any repetitive strain injuries, so go easy and don't rush things.

Being able to play several notes from a single pick stroke might sound like a good idea in terms of simple economy, but it also has an important effect on the actual sound you're creating. Despite the fact that the exercise shown above is designed to teach you to play all of the hammered notes at a single volume, whether they are picked or not, the absence of the pick attack at the beginning of each hammered note is going to remain noticeable. When a pick hits the string, the first thing that is heard is actually a burst of white noise. To you and me, all that this means is a sort of *khhh* sound, like a burst of static, and this is heard before the note itself sounds. When hammering is involved, this noise is missing. The notes may all be totally even dynamically, but the sound of the pick stroke just isn't there. So now we're dealing with two qualities of note, a plucked string sound and a hammered sound, and the two blend well to make some interesting phrases.

Consider this: you have a series of notes to play, like in the example here.

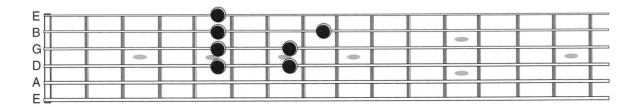

If you play each with a pick stroke before it, the result is going to be quite percussive, with plenty of attack at the beginning of each note. However, if you introduce a fair amount of hammering, an altogether different effect is produced. I've included a few audio examples on the CD which I hope will serve to illustrate what I mean.

This is really where left-hand strength comes into its own. Remember that this type of action will take time to build up into a proper-sounding technique because it's important to develop the basic muscle and co-ordination by practising repeatedly.

By practising this technique, you'll be able to adopt what we sometimes refer to as a *legato* style of playing. (*Legato* is just a fancy Italian word which means "smooth" in English.) Satriani and Vai both use this style of playing a great deal, as do the generation of players who have drawn influence from their work. However, the style is only halfway there unless we introduce the sidekick of hammering: pulling.

Pulls

Just as hammering is a way by which a player can play several notes in succession that are fuelled by a single pick stroke, pulling does exactly the same but the other way around. With this technique, your extra notes come from lifting the fingers on your left hand rather than hammering them down onto the fingerboard. In order to do this, you have to pull off the fingers from the string so that they sound the notes as they do so.

To learn a basic exercise that will help you learn this technique, go back to the seventh fret, with the third string and the third finger. This time, place your first finger on the third string at the fifth fret in readiness. This is going to be your second note, after you've plucked the string. On picking, pull your third finger off the string, exposing the one you're holding at the fifth fret. Confused? Here's a diagram.

Place first finger here   **Pluck string and 'pull off' third finger**

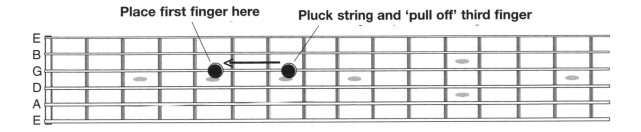

There are audio examples to back up this exercise, too, and so if you're still in the dark have a listen to the CD.

There are two schools of thought about the pull-off technique: one states that you should make a slight sideways movement with your left-hand fingertip as you pull off, so that it almost plucks the strings; the other believes that you should merely lift the finger straight off the string. My belief is that the first works on acoustic guitars and on electrics plugged into amps with low gain settings, and that the second is for electric players with a fair slice of gain to make up for an inevitable drop in dynamic as the finger is pulled off.

The end result should be the same as it was for the hammer technique: the two notes should be the same volume, and so you'll need to experiment a little in order to get things sounding right.

Hammers And Pulls Together

When used in conjunction, hammers and pulls can make a great deal of difference to a player's phrasing and can contribute greatly to the overall smoothness of the sound. Once again, it's possible to take any phrase and, if you pluck each note with the plectrum, you're going to get that initial *khhh* of white noise at the beginning of each note. By employing both hammers and pulls, you're going to smoothe out a lot of that.

If you want me to suggest a practice regimen for you to follow which will help you to get your hammer and pull techniques off the ground, I would suggest playing the scale below up and down, pulling on your way down and hammering on the way up.

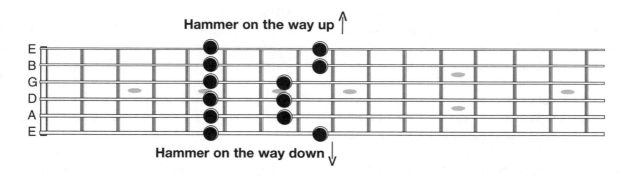

Hammer on the way up ↑

Hammer on the way down ↓

The decision when exactly to use the hammer and pull techniques – and the decision to use any of the techniques we've been studying, for that matter – is purely discretionary. There are no rules, and as such the left hand plays a vital role in developing a style. It makes you an individual.

On Developing A Style

The trick of beginning to sound individual, acquiring your own "voice" on the guitar, is something that neither a book nor a teacher can tell you; it's something which develops naturally over time. To begin with, most players model themselves on other guitarists, learning to imitate certain aspects and nuances of their playing before naturally assuming their own character at a later stage.

I don't believe that modelling yourself on another player's style can do too much harm, as long as it's done in moderation. Like anything, the minute that simple modelling turns into acute, slavish obsessiveness, something's gone

horribly wrong and it's time to pull out of the dive before it's too late. That said, however, there's nothing wrong with being influenced until it's time to flap those wings and learn to fly.

> "I was interested in the white rock and rollers until I heard Freddie King. Then I was over the moon! I knew that was where I belonged, finally." **Eric Clapton.**

> "When I heard The Blues Breakers' album, like a lot of guitarists of my generation, that was the thing which turned the world upside-down for me. When I heard that guitar, that was as powerful for me as Robert Johnson was for Eric. To hear a guitar become the main voice in the music, and to be that forceful and so direct…it was amazing. There was nothing like that before and nothing like it since." **Gary Moore.**

TRACK 20

> "When I was a teenager I was drawing my most important influences, which were the great jazz players of the Forties, Fifties and Sixties. I heard Duane and I heard Hank, but when I discovered Chet I knew that I had found my guy." **Steve Howe.**

You might not be as lucky as the players quoted above, and the moment that you find "home" as a player might not seem quite as apocalyptic. However, you can see that there is a significant weight of evidence to support the theory that it's perfectly OK to have a sort of avuncular guide to lead you towards your own style via his own. This guidance will, of course, be mute; you'll be listening to records and trying to work out what exactly is going on, and as this process continues the fruits of your research will all add up. It will lend you some of the attributes of another player's style until the day dawns when things start to come out your way, not theirs.

A great deal of a player's individuality on the instrument is concerned with basic "dialogue". In almost exactly the same way that you might build a sentence in your head while you're speaking, a player will form a musical phrase. There is eloquence in a musical phrase in the same way as there is eloquence in speech, and you can apply many of the same parameters of the latter when you can begin to play what's in your head.

I tell students that it is sometimes convenient to believe that they're actually blowing into the guitar to make the note in the same way that a wind player must. This has the effect of making musical phrases sound much more natural. Remember that melody started with the human voice, and although there have been a lot of developments since then the ear still needs certain vocal characteristics to be present in any melody it hears.

> "But the melodies are usually in my head – they are 'sung' and so they have 'breath'." **Dominic Miller.**

This is where there is a distinct advantage to singing along with yourself while you play. It helps you to keep things naturally more melodic.

LEARNING SCALES

"I think the best way to look at scales is to understand that a scale is a set of parameters that says to you 'If you follow these intervals, this is a name for that sound.' You can, of course, do anything you want to those intervals." **Joe Satriani.**

As I've said before, I think that too much emphasis is placed on the learning of scales. Too many players from the mid Eighties onwards seemed to come across like walking scale computers, and the teachers who interpreted written guitar solos from the point of view of their scalar construction have probably got a lot to answer for, too.

I actually stood next to a guy from a very famous guitar school once when he was browsing through a book of written solos. He would point to a chord symbol and say what scale would be feasible over it and then move onto the next bar and do the same thing. I realised that I just didn't think that way; I didn't want to be a scale computer, and I didn't think that it would do any of my pupils any good to become one either. Fair enough; we were both teachers from different backgrounds, with two different views on "Music: How She Should Be Taught". Occasionally, teachers will huddle in a corner and come over all academic, and I'm as guilty of this as the next guy, but I always remember something that somebody once said about analysing music being a bit like collecting butterflies – you have to kill it first in order to do so. I believe that what he meant was that taking any musical moment and pinning it down onto paper is to render that moment lost in its original form. Music that is something free and beautiful when it's heard becomes a corpse to be cut up and studied. I like to watch butterflies in flight or looning around as they do and not pinned to a piece of card in a collection, and that's how I like music, too.

Of course, some analysis is unavoidable, and it would be wrong of me to pretend otherwise; but if music can be taught in such a way that as little as possible of the original beauty is lost, and unnecessary "death" is avoided, then so much the better – at least in my neighbourhood.

Scales: An Appreciation (Ahem)

I can feel another of those "author's message" moments coming on… If you wanted me to sum up my take on studying scales and their proper, well-adjusted role in music, then it would run something like this:

Scales, like the alphabet, are a mere resource, a repository, a builder's yard of raw materials from which music is constructed. They're important, to be sure, but they're not *music*.

But don't just take my word for it…

> "The organisation of a scale is just to demonstrate to you its qualities. It's never meant to be played as music." **Joe Satriani.**

And once again:

> "There's so much more to life than scales." **John Etheridge.**

And once again, running the risk of overdoing things slightly and bludgeoning the point to death:

> "I know too many players who don't have a lot of knowledge of scales and modes, and those players tend to play from the heart more." **Dimebag Darrell.**

Three players from three different styles of music. Dimebag Darrell even mentions another of the guitar's sacred cows: modes.

So Scales Aren't Really All That Important. And Shall We Start Celebrating Now?

I think that maybe a little bit of explanation for all of this angry frothing about scales is due, and so here goes. Scales undoubtedly have great significance in music, and without doubt the study of them has its place – I would never argue with that. My concern is that some guitarists (and some of them who have become teachers) place unnecessary and wholly misplaced emphasis on them to the extent that they replace learning in other, more productive areas.

Scales are like a sort of musical alphabet: sure, you need to know (some of) them (although probably not as many as you might think), but not to the point at which they take over and dominate your life and, more importantly, the way in which you *perceive* music. If we looked at a great novel by anyone you would care to name me… Who shall we have? Dickens? Shakespeare? It doesn't really matter; I'll leave it to you to decide. Fill in your favourite great author here:................................

OK, now let's decide which was his finest work. (I could just as easily have asked you to name me any book of his that you thought was worth reading twice – it's the same thing.) Right. Now, what makes that particular novel stand out? Why did you enjoy reading it so much?

If I ask this question at guitar seminars, I usually get responses (which I may or may not choose to write on the board) such as…

"It was a good story"
"It made me feel good"
"It reminded me of when I was a kid"

…and variations on that central theme. If I then extend this to a question such as "What's your favourite song?", and quickly follow this up by asking "Why?", I usually get a very similar set of answers. In other words, in both cases people more willing to evaluate things on an emotional level than they are on an academic one. I *never*

get responses to the favourite novel question along the lines of…

"It's his use of the alphabet – it's so intense"
"His verbs, I love his verbs"
"It was a perfect example of semantics in the 19th-century novel"

…unless, that is, I've wandered into the Deconstructing Popular Literature class by mistake. Even so, I bet that the guys in that particular class appreciate the books they're discussing from an emotional point of view first and foremost – deconstruction was an academic afterthought.

So our love of guitar music and our desire to play it ourselves is really based on a set of emotional decisions rather than intellectual ones. I think that I can take for granted that we're agreed on that. In that case, why can't we approach the teaching/learning process in the same way?

> "I'm an emotional lush. I cry at *The Hunchback Of Notre Dame*, you know!"
> **Steve Vai.**

I have a final point to really ram this message home. I'm often called upon to take guitar seminars and so on, and for years I gave private tuition to many, many pupils. I found that my weak point was always providing good examples of the material we were covering in the lesson. I found it very hard to say things like "You use this scale in this way" and then come up with an example that sounded musical, as opposed to technical and "cold". Following my own diagnostic procedure, I filed this away as being a *musical* problem, although it still puzzled me why I couldn't give normal-sounding examples of the material I was trying to get across to my pupils. I put it down to awkwardness – after all, playing in an 8' x 8' teaching room is a little artificial and far from ideal.

In the end, I discovered why this problem kept arising: I simply had to "turn off teacher" – that is, I had to stop being the teacher who was concerning himself with the technical and theoretical sides of music and switch over to being a player again. As a player, I was putting emotions and feelings first instead of facts and formulae, and once I had found this important dividing line between me as a teacher and me as a player my examples loosened up a bit and became more musical.

Having said all of that, it's still difficult to give an example of a particular scale in a particular context because, speaking as a player, it's like playing with one arm tied behind your back. However, at least I've found out why I was experiencing difficulties in the first place.

I suppose that the moral here is *don't think, do*. Before you can afford to stop thinking, however, you have to learn a few things.

So What Are Scales Good For, Then?

Very glad you asked. In the same way that you can't make good concrete without combining sand, gravel, water and cement in a prescribed fashion, you can't really expect to make good music without some appreciation of its raw materials. I believe that scales are useful in two different areas:

Music Appreciation

and

Technique Building

So let's have a look at them from these viewpoints.

Music Appreciation

Remember what Joe Satriani said about scales being a set of parameters which gave you certain sounds in certain note orders? Let's examine more fully what he means.

Basically, in music you have a series of twelve notes which you repeat over and over. They start at such a low frequency that you can't hear them and they finish so high that, again, you can't hear them – but there are only twelve of them. The only thing that scales do is to subdivide these original twelve notes into sets of (usually) seven, and these sets of scales all sound different. To put it very basically, some

sound sad, some sound happy, some sound a mix of sad and happy, some sound harsh and dissonant, some sound oriental and so on and so on. All of these sounds have been given names, and so if you see something like the "Hungarian Gypsy minor" you now know that this is a sort of labelling for the sound that is created when the notes are put into this particular order. Nothing more. No further significance. Game over.

> "If you learn a few good scales then that's enough; it's much better to learn two or three really well than to learn a million and a half just so you can say that you can play the Hungarian Gypsy minor!" **John Etheridge.**

What it can also mean is that, if you found yourself in a musical situation where you needed to play something minor, Hungarian and with the spirit of a gypsy, this scale might be worth checking out because it's likely that it's been filed away for just that very purpose. If you can't ever imagine yourself being in such a position then that's no problem. Ignore it – it's not for you. However, if you're thinking "Well, I might like to check it out at some point anyway because I can't imagine what such a scale would actually sound like," good for you. An open-minded attitude like yours is a rare and beautiful thing and should be encouraged. Go raid the cookie jar.

What happened there was that you were welcoming in a bit of new musical information and prepared to make up your own mind about a new sound. That's what music appreciation is all about.

Case History

I used to teach in a few schools, and one day I decided to conduct an experiment. I gave all of the kids in the class some paper and told them to draw what they thought the music I was going to play them was about. First of all, I put on Debussy's La Mer, *and then I put on 'Mars' from Gustav Holst's* Planet Suite. *When I collected the papers later on, over half of the kids had drawn a seascape for* La Mer *and some kind of image of war for 'Mars', which is subtitled "The Bringer Of War" in the suite. I think about 60% of the twelve year olds present had "got it". They'd listened to the music, made a decision about what it sounded like to them and committed it to paper. I sometimes wonder what the kid who drew the cow is doing now, though...*

> "I think that the most useful thing that could be done in school is to put more emphasis on music appreciation so that people, whether they're going to become musicians or not, get a chance to hear music from different eras, music from different cultures, so that they have a home base of knowledge from which they can make personal decisions."
> **Frank Zappa.**

Scales break down into two main groups: the everyday and the exotic. In other words, there are scales that are very common, that you're going to meet every day of your life. You'll hear them being played in lifts, shopping malls, supermarkets and so on. I've always figured that these are the ones that you've got to know first if you want any kind of solid grounding in music, so my advice would be to go and buy a book of scales for the guitar – there are plenty around – and use it like I've already asked you to use a chord book, as a reference manual rather than as a tutor. Occasionally it might be fun to hear what some of the lesser-known scales are all about, so you can fish these out of music's musty attic and dust them off. It can't do you any harm, as long as you've told yourself that first you'll become really familiar with the "domestic" set of scales first. Exotica can wait; now it's time for the run of mill.

Without any doubt, the most common scale in music is the major scale. It's the one on which nursery tunes, pop songs and heaven only knows what else are based, and it's definitely a scale that it's necessary to know by ear. The chances are that you already know it by ear anyway, but just in case you're in any doubt it looks like this:

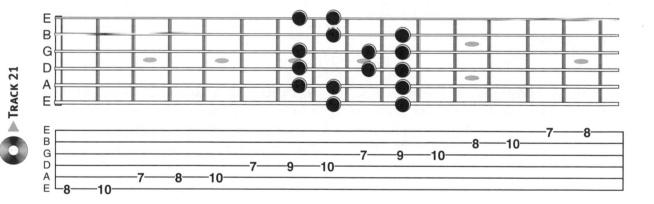

Play it to yourself a few times and try to hum it at the same time. This is the scale of C major, and it contains these notes:

C   D   E   F   G   A   B   C

That last piece of information is nowhere near as vital as it is to actually learn to hear how those seven notes sound when played in this order. Hearing is more important, OK? You've really got to know this series of notes so well that there is a subconscious reaction every time you hear music based on it. It doesn't matter if you don't get an audible *ping* and a neon "Major Scale!" sign flashing away in your head as long as you know the sound.

The next scale in line, which you need to know to exactly the same degree, is called the minor scale. It's the *ying* to the major scale's *yang*, in that it sounds more down, slightly sadder and more sombre than its major counterpart. Play it and hear for yourself:

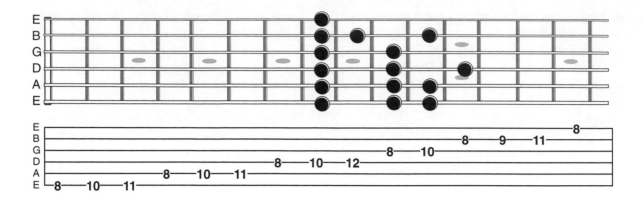

Now play this:

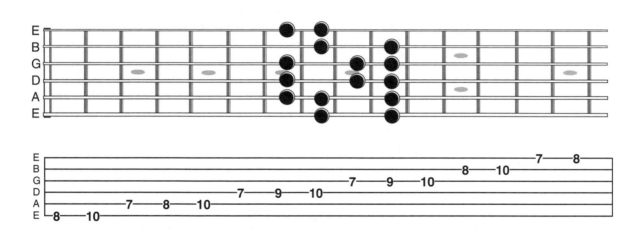

Hear the difference? This is a good basic exercise in the first stages of dragging your ear onto musical ground. You're learning to appreciate the difference between two of the most important and most commonly-used scales in music, and it's going to be of considerable help to you later on. I would recommend that you repeat this basic exercise for a minute or so every time you sit down with the guitar. Gradually the vital information will seep into your brain and you'll be in a much better position to impose your own stamp onto the music you play, based on an emotional response rather than a technical one.

Pentatonic Scales

You've probably heard these scales, although the name might not be familiar to you. As I explained previously, pentatonic scales are five-note scales which have an interesting story behind them. Fear not, I'll be brief.

As I said, virtually every culture in the world that has some kind of musical heritage (which is nearly all of them) has a pentatonic scale or two to its name. They're not really based upon each other, and they aren't that similar, but they're there, and there are African, Japanese and even Scottish pentatonic scales. The one thing that does tend to bind them, from a musicological point of view (and therefore of little interest to us here, but bear with me), is that they all function primarily in the folk culture of the respective society to which they belong. That is to say that they operate within the "natural" or endemic music, and are not particularly formalised or academic in any way. I believe that this is from where the pentatonic scales draw their power. Nobody created them as they did some of our more orthodox scale forms; pentatonic scales just *are*.

Of course, they have been dissected, studied and thence been given licence to walk in music's hallowed halls, but – to me, at least – they'll always have a slightly anarchic air about them.

Probably because of this, they feature a great deal in rock music, and especially the blues, and it's in the context of this genre that we'll be considering the pentatonic scale. There's no doubt that, without the blues, the rock and popular music that we know today would take a

very different form indeed. Remember that the blues originated as a form of African-American folk music, and its influence has touched just about every other form of music since its arrival in the Western world. You can detect the influence of blues in jazz, ragtime, country, pop, rock, swing, soul, rhythm and blues (which isn't, I admit, much of a surprise), punk, progressive, metal – have I missed anything? Musically speaking, all of these different styles of music have the simplest form of scale at their hearts: the pentatonic.

I bet you can't wait to hear one:

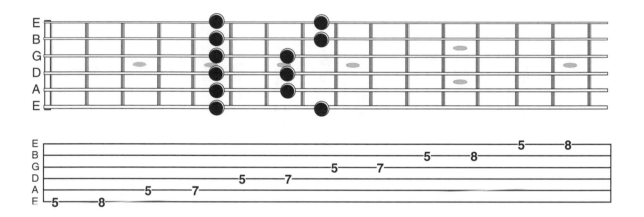

► TRACKS 22-24

If you want to know that scale's name, I can tell you that it's an A minor pentatonic, and I'd really recommend that you get to know each other well because you're about to do a lot of hanging out together.

We've seen that scales don't equal music – they're just raw material, right? – and so, taken out of context like that, you probably can't hear what all of the fuss is about, which is why I've included a couple of examples of the same scale in full battle dress, warring it out over a suitable backing track on the CD so that you can hear it in more apposite surroundings. There are also a couple of backing tracks on the disc for you to have a go at, too.

For the moment, however, I'll be talking about the minor pentatonic scale in terms of music appreciation. Become familiar with the sound of the scale so that you can weigh up your own thoughts on the matter and make an emotional judgement on it. I hope that this

judgement is of the "OK, it sounds useful enough to me, I've heard it before in music that I like, so what happens now?" variety. Otherwise it might be time for us to go outside together for a little chat…

This scale will probably be the one that you use most of all if you want to get into lead guitar playing. Even though your own particular musical journey might eventually take you towards those more exotic scales that I mentioned earlier, you'll still find that a great deal of your time is spent dallying around with these five notes. They are a very solid foundation on which to build. I think that it's pretty safe to say that most scales can be reduced to them in some form or other, and so it's a fairly simple equation to work out: pentatonic scales are the ones you need to know really well. Really, really well. Really. So I'm going to give you diagrams that will enable you to play this scale all over the fretboard.

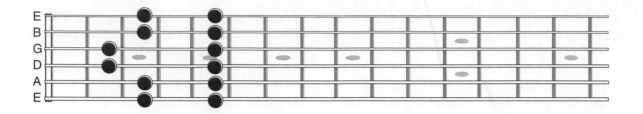

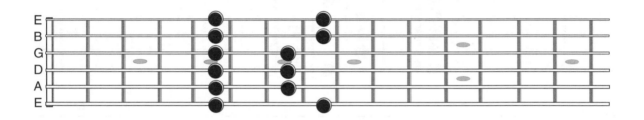

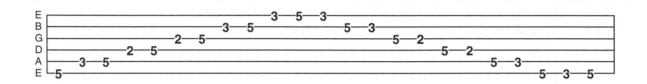

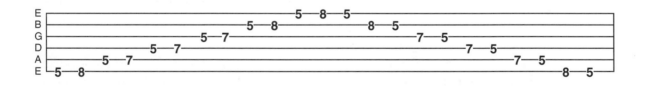

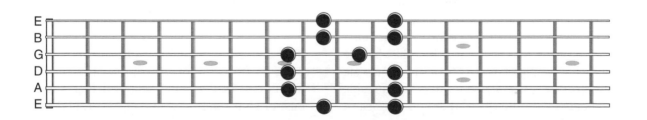

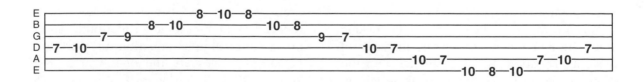

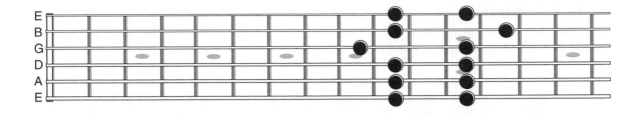

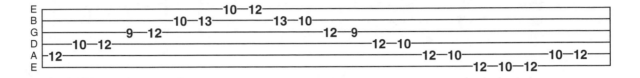

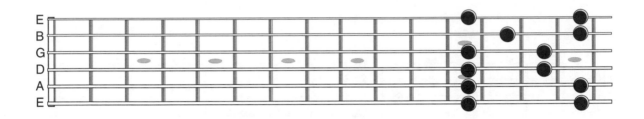

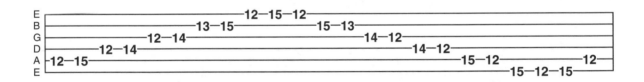

The simple exercise of playing through these shapes comes with a few rules, to which I wholly recommend that you adhere. Under each scale's "box position" I've written out the way I'd like you to play them in tab. The reason I've done this and not just thrown the whole thing open to you is that I want to help your ear develop. By playing them my way you'll be playing them all the time from A to A, beginning and ending on the key note of the scale. This will help your ear to properly tune in to the sound of the scale, and by doing this you'll be able to derive the most good from it from a musical appreciation point of view.

All that you have to do for now is play them once or twice a day each time you sit down with

a guitar. Buy a little notepad and write in it all of the things that you have to do – a practice schedule – and add to it a little every so often. In my experience, if you make a bargain with yourself and say that you've just got to spend a few minutes doing some work with the guitar before you have some fun with it (by learning a new song, or just goofing around in general), you'll accept the discipline of practice all the more readily.

Once you're playing them so that they flow, play them over the backing track so that you can hear them fit in a bit more. Remember that, all the time you're doing this, you'll also be doing your ear a great deal of good.

Theme And Variation

Having said that a great many scales are based around the one that you're learning, I'm now going to prove it to you by providing you with a couple more examples for you to play. The first example is one that you'll probably recognise immediately:

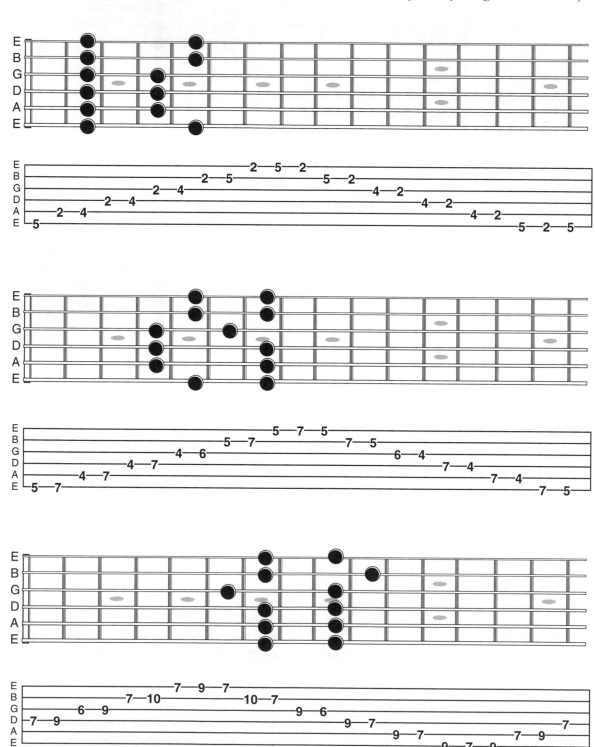

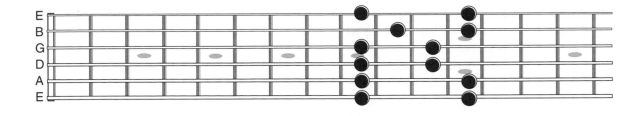

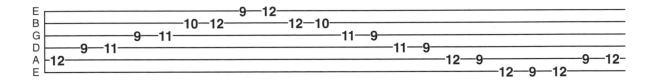

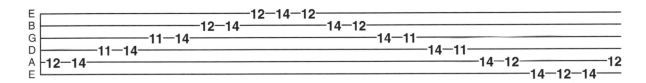

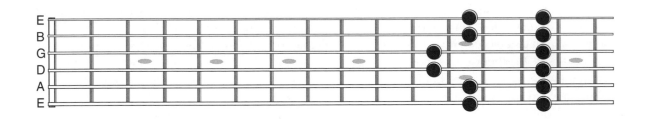

Does it look familiar? It should do because once again these are all exactly the same shapes; I've just moved them on the fretboard. This scale also has a name that isn't too dissimilar: the A major pentatonic scale. As before, I've also given you an example on the CD so that you can hear this scale as it sounds in a proper context.

You might be thinking that this scale sounds more "safe" or "nice" than the minor variation. A few of you might even be thinking that it sounds like country music, and if so you're not too far wrong. If every scale is associated with some sort of clichéd use, then in this respect the major pentatonic scale and country music sort of belong together. However, be prepared to keep an open mind about this because this scale crops up quite a lot in blues, too.

I've included tab notation again so that you can hear the scale in an optimum fashion, root

note to root note, and once again I'd advise you to play it along with the backing track once you've got it up and running.

So now you've got four scales to assimilate musically, four of the most common and most useful scales in pop and rock, and I'm just going to add one more to this list and we'll leave it at that. It's up to you to take the next step and be more adventurous with scales if your musical instincts tell you to do so. Even so, those that we've looked at here will help you play an awful lot of material, especially this next one...

> "There were scales I would hear in music and I used to think to myself 'I need to learn that scale', or 'I need to know how he got that effect using that scale with those chords'." **Kirk Hammett.**

The Blues Scale

If you needed any proof that you can't analyse art and get away with it then I'd call the blues scale as my star witness. This particular scale just doesn't exist in any real analysable form; it's a fearlessly independent thing which was born a couple of hundred years ago and worked its way into popular music by the simple means of being handed down through the generations by ear. Luckily for the blues, it wasn't recognised as anything other than the denizen of smoky, disreputable joints from which any more respectable musical form would be lucky to escape with all of its bits intact. I say lucky because in this way blues avoided going to school, and managed to grow up quite literally on the streets, fending for itself. As such, it avoided any attempts to render it down in a formula, to pin its butterfly spirit to a piece of dead card and file it away, case closed. In other words, it was a long time before the music academics got hold of it, and by the time they did it was too late – the beast lived and they couldn't subdue it.

This might sound a little dramatic, but I've been telling this basic story at seminars and in lessons for years and telling people that you can't really write the blues down on paper, and I think that that's wonderful.

As to exactly why blues has escaped the tender ministrations of the musicologists, there's a perfectly good reason and I'll tell you, in brief. Basically, the blues was a mistake. It shouldn't have happened. If it hadn't been for the somewhat alarming (and completely barbaric) practice of certain nations of visiting the west coast of Africa in the 1700s with the sole intention of kidnapping some of its population and

exporting it to the southern states of the USA as a means of securing free labour for the plantations down there, the blues wouldn't exist. Apart from the fact that it started life as the music of degradation, need, despair, hopelessness and lonely shrieking anger in response to being "relocated" by the slave traders and treated quite despicably in general, two musical forces were at work. These two opposing forces had the power to pull each other apart, but instead they found a way to evolve and combine forces, in doing so forging one of the most powerful and enduring working partnerships in modern music. This is an abbreviated version of what happened.

On the west coast of Africa in the 1700s, and long before, there was a rich indigenous music culture. Music there was tribal, powerful stuff that had been handed down through the generations by ear. Music wasn't only different to anything that was going on in the West (which we'll call the Baroque era); it also differed from tribe to tribe.

In that area, music was very local. Musicologists have found as many similarities as they have differences when studying music of this era, and it was this mixed musical heritage which travelled over the Atlantic and crashed head-on with Western music.

And what a collision it was. When African music met up with American music at that time, there were some musical pitches that didn't agree. In certain instances, African melody was slightly different in pitch and it didn't sit with some of the songs that the slaves were being encouraged to sing. The result was a completely different take on the scale. Instead of the "pure" pentatonic scale as we know it…

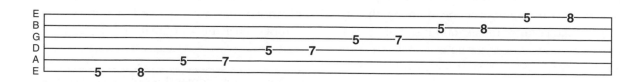

…some of the pitches were slightly sharper than is conventional. The notes concerned were these:

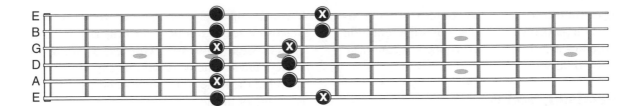

▶ **TRACK 29**

These particular notes have been referred to as being *blue notes* because it is with these that the blues really takes on its true identity. Listen to both of the above scales as they are played on the CD. Hear how the ordinary pentatonic scale only goes halfway towards being a full-blown blues statement. The blues pentatonic, on the other hand, is full of recognisable attributes. This has resulted in the blues scale, as such, being written down wrongly in guitar tutors over the years. I don't believe that you're dealing with this:

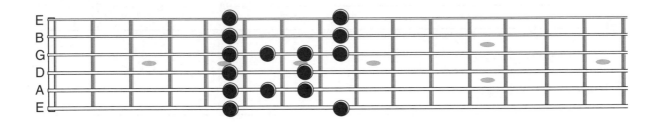

Instead, I believe that you're dealing more with this:

Bend sharp

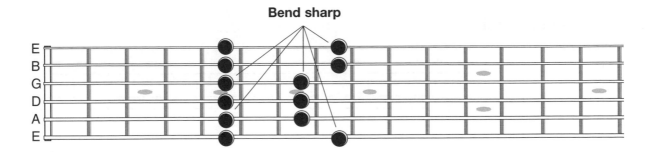

Here the indicated notes are bent slightly sharp, resulting in the sound that you can hear on the CD.

If you want to expose yourself to the aspects of this particular scale that are concerned with music appreciation, it's important that you're able to play it right. Look back to the section on lead left-hand technique if your bending skills are as yet undeveloped. Work with the blues scale with regard to the three Ps, playing it against the backing track – the flavour is all there in the notes, and it's a great musical form to practise playing music from an emotional base, too. The blues is an emotive music; when you hear a lyric like "When I woke up this morning, I found my baby gone..." we can assume that the writer wasn't having a particularly good day, and so this is a good opportunity for you to practise being as heartfelt as you can get. Let out some emotion and allow it to enter your playing – it can make all the difference.

Practising Scales

You should know by now that none of this stuff is going to filter through to you without you carrying out some work on your own, but we can still be economical about such things and make sure that you're still able to have time to have fun. In the next section we'll see how practising scales will do your fingers good, but for now we're addressing your ears, finding the correct environment for you to experience the sound of the scales for yourself and to learn the language of music.

I want you to play the following exercise at least once every time you pick up the guitar. Use it to warm up your fingers before you do anything else. (I'll be talking more about warming-up exercises soon.)

A major

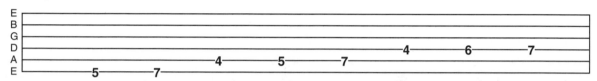

A minor

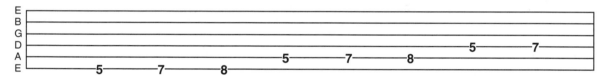

A minor pentatonic

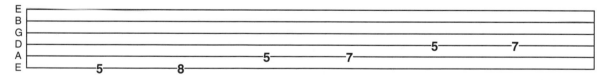

A major pentatonic

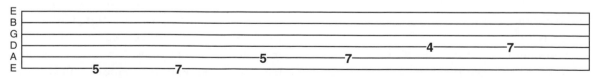

What we have here is a major scale followed by a minor, a minor pentatonic and then a major pentatonic. It's a bit like a mantra of scales, combining the most popular and common scales in the music you've set out to study. Study the blues scale as a separate entity, preferably over a backing track so that you can get the full effect.

Building Technique

With scales, the other side of the coin is pure stamina-building hard work. Remember when we separated guitar problems into musical and physical categories? Well, now that we've just addressed the musical side of the equation, this is where we get physical and teach those fingers a thing or two.

There are many hurdles to overcome with any technical development, and so before we get into things you should remember the promise that you made to yourself to shun the "can't do" barrier and avoid personal Everests, and to be true to the three Ps all the time!

Of all of the physical skills that you need to master in order to play guitar, co-ordination between the hands, flexibility, muscle development and stamina are probably the most important. They can all be mastered from the same source, too: practice. I used to write this on the board at virtually every seminar I gave:

The answer is practice.
Now, what's the question?

It raised the odd knowing smile which became more resigned as the seminar progressed and I found myself repeating the phrase (or pointing to it on the board, at least) more and more. It's so true, and I would encourage you to write it down and keep it in your guitar case so that you see it every day. Your physical development as a musician is vital, and practising is the quickest way of furthering this.

Another Equation

We could say that guitar solos are really little more than melody, right? We've also proved that melody is drawn from scales, right? Therefore, if you're going to be playing melody parts or solos (whatever you want to call them), is it not a good idea to familiarise yourself with the terrain that you'll be covering beforehand? Sure. This is where scales come in. As an exercise (and *not* as a substitute for music, please), scales will drill you in the movements that your fingers are going to make when you play melody. It will enhance your fluidity and, if done in conjunction with what we've learned about melody in general, it will aid your progress significantly. I really want to make this point absolutely clear: practice might not make perfect but it can still get you darned close.

Remember the exercise that we looked at a couple of pages back? Well, you can develop both your music appreciation and technical skills in one fell swoop, if you like. In appreciation of the fact that people don't have hours to spend practising in a world where there's always something better to do, I tried to be as economical as possible with the practice routines that I designed for my students. I wrote a book called *Guitar Workout For The Interminably Busy* (also published by Sanctuary) in order to address that fact alone, and it's a book that I'd recommend that you study if you want to explore the concept of maximum return from minimum time investment even more.

So now we're going to combine the two regimens into one. If you're going to play the "scale mantra" every time you pick up a guitar, you might as well add another factor while you're at it, and that factor is time. In every book I've written I've recommended at some point that students should go out and buy a metronome or a drum machine and use it to practise with. It will do wonders for your timing and there is no other way to achieve the same results. Timing is a serious weak spot with many guitar students, and a metronome will go a long way to improve the situation.

So now, armed with your brand-new metronome, when you sit down to recite the scale mantra you should set the metronome to an easily-achievable tempo (which will vary as you progress) and play along to its beat. For every tick, play one note. After spending a very short period of time playing along at a comfortable pace, increase the speed slightly (*personal Everest alert*: the guy said slightly, OK?) and continue for a minute or so. If you're sensible and push yourself in tiny increments you'll find that your overall technique develops nicely over a period of months.

Case History

I once had a pupil who was dissatisfied with his progress on the guitar and told me so during one lesson. He didn't feel that he was developing at all, and thought that he was stuck in a rut. I kept a record of which metronome times I set for each of my pupils and so I glanced back and set the metronome and asked him to play a scale against it. He duly (but maybe slightly unwillingly) obliged, and afterwards I told him that six weeks previously he hadn't been able to play it. He was progressing nicely but the results weren't as perceptible to him as they were to me. (I only saw him once a week.) He went home happy that day, and I started developing my theory on personal Everests then and there!

From this one exercise you can expect to derive two major benefits: by being specific in the scales you practise and by limiting them to music's most common ground you are repeatedly exposing your ear to essential information at its most basic level; and you're also systematically developing your physical playing skills, too. All of this in just one neat little package.

> "I don't think about what I do, I really don't...Put it this way: you've got this many notes – twelve notes. However you use them is up to you. None of this 'I'm playing the phrygian mode.' However you want to play them is up to you."
> **Edward Van Halen.**

Let's Be Careful Out There

One word of caution: like any repetitive physical regimen, you're exposing yourself to stress and strain on muscles and tendons (you've heard of RSI, right?), so at even the slightest sign of pain or discomfort you should stop playing immediately and rest. If the symptoms persist, you should seek medical advice.

Most problems start with bad posture, so please be sensible when you sit and practise. Don't slouch in front of the TV; try to adopt a position that you would expect to adopt while performing. Adjust the strap so that your guitar is at the same height if you're either sitting or standing, sit up straight, and keep your wrists and hands free from tension and as straight as possible. Follow these simple guidelines and you should be able to keep out of trouble.

IMPROVISING

"I tend to think in terms of colour and texture if I'm improvising. I certainly never worry about what is and isn't technically right or wrong." **Martin Taylor.**

Improvisation is a difficult thing to teach. It's very personal to each player, and it's never something that even the most experienced or fluent improviser can put into words.

For a start, I believe that everyone can improvise. They might not understand that they can, but they can. It's confusing for a lot of people to think that they'll ever learn enough about their chosen instrument – or music in general, for that matter – in order to be able to deliver something which is by nature entirely unplanned. Anyone who has spotted that this area of playing is rife with more than its fair share of personal Everests can take the rest of the day off. Alternatively, saying that you don't believe that you'll ever achieve this particular musical sleight of hand, no matter how long you practice, is another negative thought. Put it out of your mind. You *can* do it. What's more, I'll prove it to you.

Pick a subject from the list below and talk about it for 30 seconds.

Last year's holiday
My first pet
My favourite TV show
My perfect meal
A great day out
A train journey
My best friend

You don't have to talk out loud, but I bet that you could manage the task fairly easily. I mean, it was only 30 seconds, after all, and you knew your subject. You've had basic communication skills since the age of two, and so no big deal, right? Well, you were improvising, weren't you?

No one was standing behind you telling you what to say; you weren't reading from a script; and, despite the fact that you might have already told someone else much of the information you covered during those 30 seconds, you didn't do it exactly the same. Therefore, you were improvising. What's more, 30 seconds is actually quite long in terms of guitar solos. You'll probably be required to play for much less than that in a musical situation (unless you choose to play jazz, but that's a whole different ball game).

A lot of people think that musical improvisation comes from absolutely nowhere, that it's literally a hole that you must fill with no visible means by which to do it. I mean, where does it all come from, exactly? To answer that, first answer this question: what means were at your disposal when you gave your little talk in the last paragraph? As we've seen, you knew your subject.

Let's say that you chose the subject of a train journey. You'd be thinking about something quite specific; you know what a train is, you'll have travelled on one before, you know what trains are used for and that your story could be neatly bookended by some details about your departure at the beginning of your story and your arrival at the other. Fill in a few details about the scenery in between and bingo – time's up.

It's not actually that much different in a musical context. Unless you're into the rarefied area of free improvisation (in which case reading a book like this one wouldn't really apply) then we can assume that here you also have a lot of information about your subject at your disposal before you begin to improvise, or start to tell your story musically. For a start, you'll have information regarding key, harmony, rhythm, "feel", tempo, duration and so on, and that information alone is going to set up some parameters for you before you even play a note. I'll give you some idea about how these musical fundamentals could help shape your improvisation.

Key

If the given key of the piece of music – or a section thereof – is in A major, it's unwise to start playing in any other, and so your first spadeful of dirt has been dug on the way to building your foundations.

Harmony

Similarly, it's given that you will know – either by ear or by chord symbols – the chords over which you'll be expected to play. Second spadeful.

Rhythm

You're also going to be aware of the rhythmic style of the piece, too. Is it a blues shuffle, a jazzy swing, a straight 4/4? The foundations are beginning to look good.

Feel

You may be required to play over a mournful ballad, in which case certain musical events would be deemed as being ill advised, such as singing 'Roll Out The Barrel' at your aunt's funeral. Obviously, you're going to keep within certain stylistic boundaries here, too. Things are taking shape nicely.

Duration

You're going to know for how long you'll be expected to play. This will be defined by the song itself. For example, once around a set of blues changes often means twelve bars. Trenches are deep and borders are marked.

Tempo

You're going to know if the piece is slow, fast or moderately paced. You should now have a very good idea what goes where – it's really just a question of defining the "what".

So now, given that we have applied for planning permission to build an improvised guitar solo to a reasonable standard and our foundations have been finished, what's next?

Looking For Clues

Your next set of musical clues also lie in the music itself. I believe that improvisation can be looked at from three different angles:

Melody
Harmony
Relative scales

Understand that improvisation is a very deep subject, and so naturally it has attracted the attention of teams of music academics from successive generations. There are whole books on this stuff, and this is but a single chapter in a book with a fairly broad remit. Obviously we can't cover everything, but we're going to make some serious inroads.

Melody

I'm going to quote jazz guitar genius Joe Pass before we enter this particular domain:

> "It's important to know the melody of the piece you're playing…A lot of guitarists don't seem to realise that." **Joe Pass.**

How true. The melody of a piece is often overlooked by a would-be improviser because he believes that it is the very thing that he should be replacing! Playing the melody is almost anti-improvisation rather than improvisation, isn't it? Nope. Read on.

The melody of a piece of music is the true star of the show; it doesn't have to do anything except be there for people to whistle in the shower. As such it's strong enough to stand alone – people will recognise a tune from its melody but not from its rhythm or harmony. Take away the melody of a tune and it has become devoid of its main characteristic. As an example, how many people would recognise the fact that the theme to *The Flintstones* shares the same chord arrangement as Gershwin's 'I Got Rhythm'? My guess is virtually no one, unless they've studied music, and jazz in particular.

So what can the melody of a piece tell us, exactly? The answer is, just about everything. For instance, we can take for granted that the melody fits the song's harmony – its chord arrangement – like a glove, as the two mutually support each other. It therefore figures that, if the melody sits perfectly within the harmony, any improvisation based upon it will do the same. It doesn't mean that you would be expected to play the melody note for note – that would hardly be improvising – but learning to improvise around a melody is a very good place to start, and for all of the reasons that I've already listed.

You can learn to vary a melody fairly easily. First, you have to learn it. You can either do this by ear (which is the preferable method) or from a transcription (which isn't quite as good). Learning it by ear – maybe by using the method described in learning solos from records in the chapter on 'Working Out Solos From Records' – will make sure that it has entered your memory in the old-fashioned analogue fashion and not via the digital "music-by-numbers" route lent to us by tablature. Whichever way you choose to learn it, however, the melody must be really inside your head and well connected to the fingers. Ask yourself if you can hum it all of the way through without making a mistake. If you can't then you don't know it well enough yet. Return to the start and do not collect £200.

The next step is to play the melody over the harmony so that it's a perfect fit. Listen to how it sounds against the chords. Now you can begin to interpret the melody for yourself. You'll still be playing all of the same notes, but this time you can allow yourself a little artistic licence, maybe varying the lengths of some of the notes, holding a few back, playing some louder than others, playing some near the bridge to produce a bright sound and some near the neck to achieve a more mellow sound.

If you're still not entirely clear on what I mean by interpretation (and if you're still keeping a list, I hope you've added it to the *musical* category of problems!) then you should conduct a little research. Get hold of two or three versions of the same song by different singers (it doesn't even have to be the one on which you're working – the lesson can still be learned this way around) and listen to how the tune has been interpreted differently. One example is the difference between Peter Green's and Carlos Santana's versions of 'Black Magic Woman'. Peter's version is vocal, with a fine solo based on the melody of the piece, whereas Carlos' version is an instrumental with even more melodic variation involved. Beginning to get the picture?

If you're practising this kind of thing you might feel a little insecure about moving away from the melody at all. After all, where do you go from here? Which notes will sound right? This means that it's time to do a little more research – it's all practice, and it's all necessary. You wouldn't be alone in your studies…

> "I spent all of my mid to late teens and early 20s studying the music, studying the geography of it, the chronology of it, the roots, the different regional influences and how everybody inter-related and how long people lived and how quickly they learned things and how many songs they had of their own and what songs were shared around. I mean, I was just into it…I was learning to play it as well and trying to figure out how to apply it to my life. I don't think I took it that seriously because when we're young we don't. It was only when other people showed an interest that I realised I could make a living out of it."
> **Eric Clapton.**

Using the melody as a basis for improvisation is a little like learning how to swim. It's very easy to get out of your depth, and for a while at least you may feel too timid to let go of the side of the pool and leave the melody for deeper musical waters. It's understandable, but this is exactly what practice is for. There's also the added bonus that, with the guitar at least, you don't have to get wet, cold and you get to keep your clothes on.

Safe Notes

So how do we let go of the edge of the pool and take our first few strokes into this strange world of melodic improvisation? For a start, you need to know where the safe notes are – and before you all start grumbling that I'm giving you even more work to do, relax because you already know the safe notes. You know them because they're the other notes in the melody. Now, this system isn't 100% foolproof, but then what system is? The chances are high, however, that the other notes of the melody will fit quite nicely over the chord changes, and so that's where your basic database of notes can be formed.

There's a reason for this, of course, and I'll tell you because some of you will want their curiosity satisfied. If you don't, skip this paragraph. Usually, the notes of a melody stick pretty faithfully to a single scale (about which more in a moment). The chord arrangement

will most likely stick to a single key, unless you're playing jazz (sorry to keep mentioning jazz all the time, but it is a special case), and so the melody and harmony of a piece will be linked by a very common theme: key and scale. They fit each other so well that most of the time notes from the melody can be quite happily mixed up a bit over the same chordal backing to form other melodies, like guitar solos for example. In fact, that's pretty much all a guitar solo ever is.

If you've skipped that last paragraph then I hope that you'll reconsider reading it at some point – there was some really good stuff in there.

So you're now in a position where you can play a song's melody over the chords. It's now time to vary the melody a little and have a go at improvising. I advise you to get yourself a blank-neck diagram like this one:

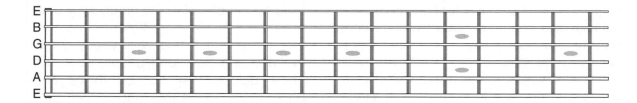

Now write down all of the notes from the melody onto the diagram. Play them one at a time and then put them all together on your diagram. What you have now is your database of safe notes for this particular song. Play the song again over a backing track and put some extra notes in, or leave some out. Play anything you like, as long as you don't simply play the melody again note for note. You've got to let go of it at some point.

It's important that you shouldn't be entirely random in your choice of substitution; don't act like a computer program would and have absolutely no basis from which to choose your notes. Instead, listen hard. Choose notes close to those from the melody – literally play around them. If your ears are developing in the way that they should be by now, you should find that you're able to come up with a few perfectly

reasonable ideas with which you can construct solos. It may be the case that they still don't sound as adventurous as John Scofield does in full flight, but nevertheless you'll have taken that important first step in improvisation and played something that wasn't in the tune when it first left the composer's pen. The chances are that, when we've looked at the other two ways by which you can approach improvisation, you'll feel confident enough to brave the deep end of the music pool.

> "I remember asking my father what Django Reinhardt was doing when he took a solo, and he told me that all Django was doing was playing a variation on the song's melody with notes of his own choosing…That really opened a few doors for me." **Martin Taylor.**

Harmony

> "The most dangerous thing is improvising with a band and thinking 'Okay, now's the time to play that diminished scale'…and somebody in the band is thinking 'Now's the time to play that major chord.' Those kinds of accidents do happen." **Frank Zappa.**

Another path into improvisation is via the song's chord arrangement. The relationship between a song's melody and its chord arrangement is very strong, and it provides us with one unassailable guarantee: there are no wrong notes in there. In other words, if you're playing your own substitute melody (or guitar solo) over a chord arrangement, and you're playing notes from the chords themselves, then you can't go wrong. You're on safe ground, just as you were when you were playing notes that were contained in the song's melody.

Basing your improvisation around a song's chord arrangement is a tradition almost as old as improvisation itself. It is, for instance, the way in which a lot of traditional jazz improvisation is wrought, even today.

> "I think a lot of the emphasis on scale study is slightly misplaced, especially when it comes to playing over changes. Something I always mention is that jazz improvising employed no scales until the middle Sixties. That's when rock and jazz improvising started merging and became scalar. It was John Coltrane and Miles Davis who, in the late Fifties, started using scales as opposed to chord tones." **John Etheridge.**

It could be argued that simply knowing a song's melody isn't knowing the song itself. There's much more to it than that. If you're going to perform a song with a band, it's safe to assume that you should also know the chords; if you don't, consider the job only half done. As you already know them, we might as well make use of the chords in our improvising gambit, too.

There are basically two ways in which to play a chord: as a block (that is to say that all the notes are strummed in such a way that they sound simultaneous, which is a feat that is almost impossible on the guitar, if you think about it, but still), and one by one (which is technically known as an *arpeggio*). To make things neat and simple – and so that you can quite safely forget the word I've just taught you – we'll say that they're either strummed or picked.

Strummed

Picked (an arpeggio)

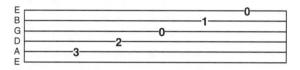

When you pick each note of a chord in this way, you are still functioning in an accompanying role, of course. You're still playing the chords; you're just playing them differently. If the melody wasn't there, the chords might not sound quite enough to make the song work, but it would still be pleasant enough to hear. We can assume that, if the chords are that important to a song's structure (and without doubt they are), we can make use of them for the purposes of improvisation.

Before we move on any further, we'd better just have a quick look at chords, just to make sure that everyone knows exactly what's going on. A chord is, by definition, usually three notes played simultaneously. The choice of note is far from arbitrary, and the way in which a chord is made up is covered in the chapter on 'Learning Chords' earlier in the book. If you're not sure, or if you're the type who reads books from the middle, then by all means go back and look at the explanation there. I covered the basics in that chapter, but now I have to take you a little further. We shan't be covering anything too technical, and it's definitely going to be of use to you, so I would invite you to bear with me for a couple of paragraphs while we delve further into the mysteries of the chord.

Chords are really just notes from a musical scale put together to support a melody. I always tell pupils to imagine a fence, the horizontal parts of which represent the melody and the vertical posts the chords, or harmony. In fence terms, you could say that many fences come from the same basic material, wood, and that one part of a fence supports the other.

The same is true in music. As we've seen before, chords are common to just about every kind of music. You'd be using the same basic chordal ideas if you were playing country, rock, jazz, blues, classical or nearly any other type of guitar-related music that you can name. The exceptions – before anyone points them out or starts mailing me – would be plainsong, or Gregorian chants, which are types of music that are pretty much devoid of harmony as we recognise it today.

However, chords are chords, whether they're played by a rock band or by an orchestra. They're still made up in the same way, and they still fulfil the same basic function.

If we take a scale of C major…

C D E F G A B C

…and then look at what notes are contained in a chord of C major…

C E G

…and then look at where they are in that scale…

C D E F G A B C

…then you might begin to see the relationship between the two. If we try the same trick again with a different scale, we should just about have the whole thing sewn up.

Let's try D major this time:

D E F♯ G A B C♯ D

Look at the notes in the following chord:

D F♯ A

Now highlight their position in this scale:

D E F♯ G A B C♯ D

You can see a system beginning to develop here, can't you? All chords are made up in this way, but we're not going to get any more technical, except than to make this final point.

Back to the fence analogy. If the horizontal bit of the fence (the melody) is made up from the C major scale, then the vertical posts (the chords) are, too. Hopefully, you can see how this happens from the examples above.

At this point, I will say that this is not by any means a rule which is set in stone. Of course not; nothing's that simple, especially in the somewhat wacky world of music. However, this is a rule which applies in general, and, for the purposes of understanding how chords can be used to help with improvisation, it's a very good model on which to work.

Chordal Improvisation

In order to show you how this particular trick works, I've included some examples on the CD. I'm not about to transcribe exactly what I played because I want you to learn this lesson by ear and by experimentation, and so there are some backing tracks as well with which you can practise.

Basically, we have a bluesy chord arrangement in the key of A, and in order to get this point across I'm going to be really specific about which chord shapes I want you to use. If these shapes look new or unfamiliar to you, take them at face value for now and look up why they are what they are as part of your own studies later on.

▼ **TRACKS 30-31**

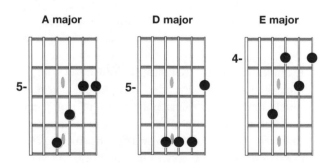

Here's the chord arrangement, which is basically a twelve-bar blues pattern using only major chords, if you want me to be specific here for a moment.

| Amaj / / / | Dmaj / / / | Amaj / / / | Amaj / / / |

| Dmaj / / / | Dmaj / / / | Amaj / / / | Amaj / / / |

| Emaj / / / | Dmaj / / / | Amaj / / / | Amaj / / / | |

The first example you'll hear on the CD is the chord arrangement on its own, just to set the scene. This should also help you to focus your ear on the harmony of the piece.

The next section is me playing only the notes of the chords themselves over the backing track, so for the A major sections I'm playing this chord shape but in single notes:

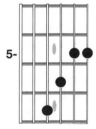

How did it sound to you? If your answer was "Melodic, but not really very interesting" then you get to go home early with a gold star. The reason why it didn't sound very interesting was because I limited my melodic endeavours to a very small range of notes, just the ones contained in the chord and nothing more. If I add some other notes, the whole thing becomes a little more exciting. Listen to the next example on the CD.

This time I included some other notes which are not found in the chords, and I expect you're going to demand to know where I got them from. As a matter of fact the extra notes were from the A minor pentatonic, but they could have come from the song's melody (if it had one) because it's likely that this would have been from where the song's melody would have been drawn anyway. The idea of using scales as a basis for improvisation is what we're going to look at later in this chapter, but for now just listen to the CD examples and play around with them yourself against the backing tracks.

▲ TRACK 32

▲ TRACKS 33-34

> "This whole thing of learning to improvise via chord scales is very useful but it can be deceiving. All seven notes of a scale are not equal – some are definitely stronger than others – so I encourage people to play entire solos only using chord tones and not using any approach notes or scale notes at all, but only using the three or four basic notes of whatever the chord is." **Pat Metheny.**

Metheny's advice here is extremely sound. After all, we've proved how you can't possibly go wrong if you play improvised passages made up from chord tones. However, you might have noticed that he's hinting that chordal thinking is preferable to thinking about which scale fits which chord, and we haven't looked at that particular strand of information yet. My own take on the situation is that good improvisation, the stuff that really works, is made up from all three methods combined into one: from the melody, from the chords and from the relevant scales. Now let's look a little more at how scales feature in the guitarist's world.

Scalar Improvisation

If I might be allowed to get up on my soap box for a few moments again here, I must tell you that I think that the guitar student's pre-occupation with scales in improvisation is all wrong. And I'm not alone…

> "I can always tell if I guitarist is playing a solo based solely on using the 'appropriate scales' principle. It sounds unmusical, like he was using a slide rule instead of his heart." **Martin Taylor.**

I believe that a lot of damage was done during the Eighties and early Nineties by the emphasis that was put on guitar students – particularly rock guitar students – to learn scales. They learned them well, and they learned to play them fast, but scales aren't music in the same way that the alphabet isn't literature. It's a source, a means to an end, but it's definitely no substitute for teaching yourself to think melodically rather than as some kind of scale thesaurus crossed with a mathematician.

> "The point is, if you're playing over a lot of changes and you think of chord tones, it's easier to get around things because you've got the visual shape of the chord on the fingerboard, and that's how people like Joe Pass played." **John Etheridge.**

This is why I have left the section on scalar improvisation until last, because I wanted to shift its importance down a few notches and give you some time with which to see the benefits of learning to think from a more melodic point of view.

I'm not saying that scales are unimportant, or that you should avoid learning them at all costs. Far from it. I've illustrated what kinds of benefits you can expect to enjoy from practising scales, but in many ways the practise room is the best place for them. Use them to get your fingers accustomed to moving over the fretboard, use them to help your ear detect some of music's different sounds, buy a book with loads of them in and occasionally dip into it to learn some new sounds, but please don't try to use them as a substitute for melody. Do we have a deal?

> "Even though these scales exist, it's not really how to play music. It's just playing scales, and I think the emphasis on the scales is a little too strong." **John Scofield.**

The idea of scalar improvisation is really fairly simple…to begin with. In fact, I'm not going to let it become too complicated because that isn't why we're here. There are plenty of resources out there which you can draw on to obtain all of the information that you require on which scale goes with which chords. I'm only going to show you how the basic idea is put together.

The reason why the minor pentatonic scale works so well over blues is that it's packed full of chord tones, the notes with which you can't possibly go wrong with. Let's start by looking at this example:

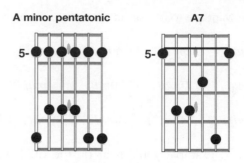

A minor pentatonic   A7

Do you see the similarity here? When we talked about chordal improvisation a while ago, we found that playing on chord tones was one sure way of playing a solo, even if it was a little unadventurous. This is certainly the case here; the chord of A7 is neatly outlined in the scale, and there are even a couple of non-chord tones that you can use for variety. It's no coincidence that this is by far the most popular scale with guitarists. It's a sort of "do anything, go anywhere" sort of affair that's extremely durable and quite easy to play. Few consider why this should be so, but that's not really the point: it works, end of story. However, if we can use chord tones to fit over a chord, can we do the trick the other way round and find a scale which fits a chord? Of course we can.

If you think back to the section in which we examined where chords come from a couple of pages ago, you'll remember that a chord is really just three notes of a scale which kind of sum up the scale when they're played together. The whole essence of C major can be summed up by using only three of its notes: C, E and G. It's an abbreviation; it sums up "C-ness".

So if we find a C chord cropping up in a piece of music a number of times, are we free to use the scale of C to improvise over the top? You bet. In fact, that's really all there is to it, but you might want to know a little bit more, just for luck.

Let's take a song in the key of C and examine the chords in a bit more detail. The chords in this key are most likely to be these:

C major   F major   G major

To explain exactly why this is the case would be to take us too far down the dark corridors of learning with nought but a candle, so for now just take my word for it. Having established our chord arrangement, let's put the chords themselves under the microscope and have a good look. Breaking down each chord into their three notes apiece gives us this:

C major: C E G
F major: F A C
G major: G B D

Take a good look at the notes contained in those chords. If we lay them end to end, we get something like this:

C E G F A C G B D

If we rearrange them into the musical alphabet (and ignore the fact that there are two Gs), we get this:

C D E F G A B C

Which is the scale of C major. Good trick, huh? So now you should be thinking that this would mean that you can use the C major scale to improvise over the entire chord arrangement, and you'd be dead right. Over each chord, we've got the basic requirements for an interesting improvisation: chord tones, plus a few scale tones to make things more interesting. When the C chord is being played, we have this arrangement:

C D E F G A B C

When the accompaniment changes to F major, we have this:

C D E **F** G **A** B **C**

When things turn towards G major, this happens:

C **D** E F **G** A **B** C

The formula stays the same each time: chord tones, plus some scale notes for added interest. Therefore, if you practised your C major scale until you were competent and speedy with it, you could safely blast away over this chord arrangement with

all the sure-footedness of a mountain goat. *But* (and here comes another one of those "author's message" things) it would still sound like a scale being played randomly over a chord arrangement if we didn't acknowledge the fact that the chord tones change all the time, giving us a different set of absolutely safe notes at each chord change.

This is where a lot of players go seriously wrong. They play their C major scale as fast as biology will allow with absolutely no regard for the song's melody or the chordal centres of gravity. In other words, everything comes out sounding very athletic but not particularly melodic or tuneful, and that's contrary to the whole point isn't it? We should be seeking to replace the melody of the song with an alternative melody.

It's a system that works even in the most oddball situations. The band Steely Dan (well, Walter Becker and Donald Fagen, anyway) have been confounding people for years with their chord arrangements, over which it's defiantly difficult to solo. They are full of sudden twists and turns, harmonically speaking, which make for a difficult time if you happen to be in the position of playing a guitar solo over them. However, as we're often told, attitude is everything. Here's how Steely Dan guitar veteran Rick Derringer deal with their chord charts:

> "They have charts with pretty much everything written out, and sometimes it's challenging, but on the other hand it's always pretty much a blues, so the challenge of those charts can put you off the simple reality which exists there. But they are pretty ornate changes around the blues." **Rick Derringer.**

The basic blues chord changes are far from unique to the blues; they permeate music itself. If you take a look at what's actually going on in terms of harmony, the blues share a basic similarity with many, many pieces of music, so learning blues is an almost perfect way of training yourself up to cope with other areas of music which could be more harmonically dense. This isn't the first time that I've heard someone offer the advice to treat everything as a blues.

I once had the pleasure of spending some time with the great jazz guitarist Tal Farlow. He was writing out the set list for that night's performance and I happened to remark that one particular jazz standard always gave me problems while soloing. "Why?" he asked me. I said that the changes were so remote and seemed so unconnected that it was difficult to play anything which really fitted. He just smiled and said:

> "Just bend it to make it fit." **Tal Farlow.**

For a long time I didn't know what he meant, but he was basically telling me to play in such a way that I could use the difficult changes by playing in a way with which I was familiar and just moving things aside occasionally to make the improvised melody fit the shape of the song. The same way, in fact, that Rick Derringer dealt with Steely Dan.

Therefore, in my book, the only solid basis for improvisation that works as far as your audience is concerned (and if you're not playing for them then you should ask yourself who you're actually playing for) is a combination of the three approaches that we've been considering: think about the song's melody, use the chord tones as sonic landmarks and make use of the scales involved to add interest.

Inspiration

While we're here, we'd better answer the most frequently-asked question about improvisation that there are: "What exactly do you think about while improvising?" The best way I've found to answer this is to pose another question: "What were you thinking about when you asked that question?" Most people reply "Well, nothing. I was just asking a question." That's about as much sense as you can expect to get out of a guitar player who is a renowned improviser – they're not thinking about anything, they're just playing.

> "When you're improvising and you're trying to think quickly and clearly, you don't want a lot of clutter in your head." **John Etheridge.**

In a way, you could say that experienced musicians who are good improvisers are just so sufficiently well versed in the language of music that they have no problem in communicating with the rest of the world in that way. In exactly the same way that some people are gifted public speakers, some musicians have the power to channel that same eloquence into their music.

But where does all of this leave us? As you can imagine, there's no easy way to teach someone how to be a seamless improviser; it has to come from somewhere within.

> "When I was at art school, one of the teachers said that, whenever you make a mark, you have to review every other mark you've made, and I think the best music is made like that. Unfortunately, a lot of people don't have time for that and end up with the verse, verse, chorus, change key, go home approach." **David Rhodes.**

> "I find the best ideas come from when you're not actually touching the guitar, otherwise your fingers fall into the same positions and you get stuck in the ruts." **Brian May.**

Phrasing

> "Guitar players might listen to a guy like Mark Knopfler and say 'Well, he's not doing anything special,' but listen to the guy's phrasing and that's partly why audiences love to listen to that stuff." **John Etheridge.**

> "Phrasing is a difficult thing to teach, which is why people will teach harmony, because you can systematise it. You can't do that to phrasing; you just have to advise them to think about it, leave spaces, use rhythmic devices, don't play on the beat all the time – things that will make even a trite little scale passage sound more interesting. And the whole point is to create interest when you play; you're trying to get people to listen to you." **John Etheridge.**

All I can advise you to do, on the subject of phrasing and generally achieving a high level of eloquence on the guitar, is to make sure that you put in enough time in the research lab. Be careful not to kill the butterfly but watch it in flight by listening with an open mind to as much music by as many different players as you can. When you hear something that works, or in some way speaks to you, try to imitate it; find a transcription, study it and find out what makes it tick. Store this information away carefully, learn the right lessons from it and try to bring as much of it to your own playing as you can. One day, all of the knowledge that you'll have accumulated will blend together, and the result will be an almost unconscious reading of it, a blend of ideas from all across the musical spectrum which have been filtered through your own unique personality into something fresh, exciting and beautiful.

BUILDING A SOLO FROM SCRATCH

"The best solos often come from the best songs, when you've got something to feed off." **Brian May.**

This chapter is intended to be primarily audio in content, and so the bulk of it is included on the CD, but I also thought that I should still include some by-the-by information here.

We've already looked at a lot of things which are going to help you in this area, and by now you know my catechism about how fast, flashy scales do not equal music.

Here, however, our brief is different to the one we followed when we were considering solos that were wholly improvised. We're now concerned with the composed solo, which may stand as an integral part of a song or an instrumental. Of course, it has to be said that many written guitar solos often began life as several improvised attempts in a studio, the end result being a kind of patchwork quilt of all of the best improvised bits strung together; but how does this differ significantly from the process of composition? In my book, not very much; it's merely a different means to the same end.

I remember being very surprised the first time I saw some of the instrumental guitar giants of the Eighties, at how many of the guitar parts that I believed to be improvised solos were actually played as written. I was astounded that Joe Satriani played things almost note for note live, including the parts that I had assumed were originally improvised on the recording. However, if improvisation is instant composition (as it is often described), there is indeed a link between the improvised and composed solo.

There are many views on what makes a good solo. In order to help you form your own, try out this simple exercise. I used to ask pupils to name me their top three favourite and least favourite guitar solos. This would give me a clue as to their

tasted and favoured playing styles. All of the solos on both *good* and *bad* lists were linked somehow; sometimes the bad list comprised solos which they considered technically inept or inappropriate, out of context to the song, and here they had spotted the first generalisation that is often made:

The solo has to represent the song in some fashion

If it doesn't fit stylistically then why is it in there? Remember that, in a recording studio, there is always a second chance to play a take again, and while we may be inclined to forgive a glorious botch job on the stage, patching up a mistake in the studio is as easy as saying "roll that tape again".

Other conclusions which were common to the *bad* list concerned sloppy technique. Now, this is a very personal area which is subject to almost infinite interpretation, and we could get into talking about how even primitive art still qualifies in the grand plan of things. However, like I said, we are dealing here with a very subjective area, and the only thing that's really certain – and the only judgement which any of us are really qualified to make – is whether we like something or not. With this in mind, by all means come up with a list of your least favourite solos of all time and find the common thread, cordoning off that area of in your mind as a no-go zone, but don't deny others access!

Usually, when I looked at students' *good* solo list they were all somehow thematically linked, too. Often favourite solos were by favourite guitarists and were very similar in style, and there's nothing wrong with that, either. It's an expression of personal taste, that's all. Quite often, however, when I asked them exactly why they liked a particular solo, I'd get very similar responses:

It's exciting
You can hum it
It just lifts the song
It's all the right notes in the right place
It sounds so powerful
It just works, somehow

Things like that. If we allow ourselves to draw conclusions from this list, we might deduce that the perfect guitar solo is exciting, memorable, effective, well conceived, well played and well structured. As a generalisation, I think you'll find that this summing up probably applies to your own list, too.

However, we're not here to analyse structure from a dreary academic point of view. We've managed to avoid it so far. I mean, academics really fell into a trap they'd dug for themselves when some herbert proved that a bumble bee couldn't possibly fly because the ratio of its body weight to its wing span was all wrong. Well, the bumble bee community has so far not commented on the revelation. They've probably been too busy flying about on matters of dear import.

Sometimes, it's just a better idea to leave the slide rule at home and appreciate things for what they appear to be. Good music is good no matter what. Why try to analyse all of the beauty out of it?

> "The guitar, through being a lesser instrument in terms of repertoire, suffers even more from a very precious, rather pretentious, over-particularised book of rules in terms of interpretation. Most of the criticism you read of performances and things like that don't mean anything. You often read about the way so and so controlled their tone in the transition from the first to the second subject, and the beautiful transparent textures in the change from G♭ major to...whatever, when all they're really saying is that they played it really nicely!" **John Williams.**

So if we're not going to build a solo by actually deconstructing and studying others – a route which is wide open to you via books already available in the marketplace – then how are we going to make a start? I think that we can afford to take the analogy route in many ways and look at things like shape and dynamics. Here are a few ideas I've picked up over the years which you could mull over before attempting any of the practical work on the CD.

• A good guitar solo should tell a story; it should have a beginning, a middle and an ending.

• Imagine that you're telling a joke, and build up to the punchline.

• Remember that you're playing for an audience, and most people want to be entertained instead of bludgeoned senseless with a barrage of notes.

• Don't use it as an excuse to play everything you know. This is commonly referred to "dumping your trickbag".

• Don't be precious about ideas. If something doesn't work, drop it and file it away for use in the future.

• Try to picture the space you have to fill, either in musical terms – such as how many bars, etc – or more allegorically, like a box that you need to fill with notes. Try to make what you play fit perfectly.

• Remember that a good, emotionally-based guitar solo is nearly always more memorable than a purely technical one

If anyone is still puzzled by how a solo should have a "shape", and why you should need a "rule of thumb" or a "fail-safe" process in order to get started, try starting your solo down the low end of the fretboard, playing sparsely and working up in both intensity (ie playing more notes) and pitch (playing higher notes). Playing an ascending, gradually-intensifying musical passage is the easiest way of creating excitement and tension.

You can look for ways to implant emotion in a solo in some really surprising ways, and I often cite film music as a good example. It's audio/visual – you can see what's going on, so you don't have to imagine it – and the brief of the movie composer is always to enhance what's going on in a scene. Think about the soundtrack to a horror film. The axe murderer (no pun intended) is climbing up the stairs to the bedroom in the dark house… What's the music soundtrack doing at this point? Is it building tension in some way? How? Write down what you *feel* is happening and experiment over one of the backing tracks to see if you can include those elements in a solo yourself.

Another analogous method is to keep something focused in your mind – a shape, an event, a picture, a sunset, anything – and try to sum it up with the notes you play. If you think that this is at all an odd way of going about things, listen to a good, earthy blues guitar solo and tell me that there's no emotion behind it. If you're singing about hardship and hopelessness, you've got to try and superimpose those emotions on whatever you're playing.

"I start off looking for what I think is the tempo of the particular section I'm working on, what feels right, and that can take a couple of hours, experimenting. You may start with a click track and then maybe try playing a few things to it and find that it isn't going to sit. When you do find something that works, you start building it up from there. That's where it is similar to doing something for Peter [Gabriel] because we will invariably start with a groove and then find something to play against it. I may end up losing the groove, but I always go for that first. The way Gabriel always works is that he's after the groove; he may have the melody, but then we'll work really hard to get things sitting nicely, and once you've done that it's much easier to find the lines over the top." **David Rhodes.**

So how would you like your solo? Smokin' or non-smokin'? We can make that the first decision:

are we playing over a sensitive ballad or over a down-home rock song?

The next thing to consider is how the whole thing can be built from small sections. Consider the idea that a good solo tells a story. Now think of what makes up a story from a technical point of view. If we were to make a list it might look something like this:

Letters
Words
Sentences
Phrases
Paragraphs
Punctuation
Narrative

That could translate into:

Notes
Phrases
Dynamics
Themes
Flow

In order to begin putting our solo together, we're going to acknowledge Rick Derringer's Steely Dan theory that everything is basically blues, and the bits which don't follow this basic pattern you merely adapt – you'd bend them to fit, as Tal Farlow put it. Rick's theory is actually quite sound, from a theoretical viewpoint. If you want proof, I'll have to put on a technical hat for about a paragraph.

The basic chord structure of the blues takes the form of three basic chords. In C, these would be:

C   F   G

The only difference you'd notice if we were going to play a blues in the down-home, baby-done-left-me sense would be that each of these chords would belong to the family of sevenths and would look like this:

C7   F7   G7

Musically, these chords are very similar in structure, with the sevenths having an extra note each, like this:

```
C = C E G       C7 = C E G Bb
F = F A C       F7 = F A C Eb
G = G B D       G7 = G B D F
```

Now, this three-chord idea isn't peculiar to the blues; it runs throughout tonal music, irrespective of style. Even hymns share similar characteristic to the blues, believe it or not, and it's certainly true to say that a lot of pop and rock music takes this basic structure as a foundation. In terms of scales, you can get by with the good old pentatonic scale over a blues pattern, which we've already seen, but it will also do very nicely over the basic chord structure as detailed above.

So my equation runs like this: if this basic chord structure runs throughout a lot of the music over which you might be expected to play (and we've already looked at a scale that fits it quite nicely), why not take each chord individually, work out some phrases to suit and then try putting them together in a sort of graduation piece at the end? In this way you'll learn to be fairly sure footed as you negotiate popular music's common ground.

The backing tracks run like this: first of all you have three tracks which stay on a single chord almost interminably. This is to give you a chance to build up a catalogue of little phrases which fit over the chord.

The chords are in the key of A, and so the first chord is A, the second is D and the third is E. The A minor pentatonic scale will fit over each of the chords, but you will sense a shift in the priority of notes when you play over the D and E chords. This is doing your ear no end of good, because this is the most natural way of learning to play over chord changes without resorting to a purely technical route. I want you to be able to hear chord changes rather than simply respond to a given set of rules.

The next set of backing tracks combines the chords of A and D. This will be your opportunity to combine phrases from the A and D sections and to make the transition sound natural and thematic. You'll hear both chords for an equal length of time, and once again the track will play for long enough to ensure that you don't have to keep getting up and pressing the repeat button.

Next there is a track which swaps between the

three chords in equal measures to add the responsibility of handling all three at once. Again, try to link them thematically; try to anticipate the change, feel where it's going to happen and switch over from your A phrases to D and E phrases as naturally as you can.

Once you feel able to do this, I've recorded a basic chord arrangement which follows the structure of a blues, using all three chords. This will give you a chance to play a fully-fledged solo over what I hope is a familiar-sounding chord structure.

Finally, there is a backing track which employs all three chords without an underlying blues structure, so you won't be able to anticipate the chord changes at first. You're going to have to feel your way through it, dipping into your stock of licks cautiously at first and then with growing confidence as you learn to hear the chord changes.

This kind of learning regimen is not uncommon, *although I'm not going to write down the chord sequence for the final example*. This is a vital step that must be taken in order to allow your instincts to develop naturally and to teach you to *listen* and *respond*.

Basic Guidance

> "The idea of creating melody from scratch based on an ostinato or single chord that doesn't change – that was the world that I felt most comfortable with." **Frank Zappa**.

In order to help you build up a stock of phrases over each chord, keep a notebook of your best licks written out in tab and update and rewrite them all the time.

> "My tunes tend to evolve out of me practising. They don't really evolve out of me writing as such because I write a bit, I record some things, I look back at them, I update them, I lengthen them, I fix them with other bits, but there is a time when it comes together, and that was when 'Clap' came together." **Steve Howe**.

▼ TRACK 41   ▼ TRACK 42

▲ TRACKS 35-38

▲ TRACKS 39-40

Be quite self-critical in what you keep in your book. This will ensure that your library of phrases represents your best work.

> "I throw away probably ten ideas to every one I keep. The song has got to make me feel good before I can hope to turn anyone else on to it." **Peter Frampton.**

You'll find that your best ideas come to you naturally, when you're not actively thinking about what you're doing. This allows for an element of chance to inspire you to play differently.

> "Occasionally there's a happy accident which leads me in a nice direction." **Brian May.**

Eventually you'll develop a database of licks on which you can call when you're jamming or improvising, but the above exercise will teach you how to come up with phrases more and more spontaneously until you don't even have to think too much about what you're doing – the music will begin to flow freely. At this point you can test yourself on the gig circuit.

> "I start [writing] a song and I don't know where it's going to end up. When I start writing I let the song lead me astray!" **Steve Hackett.**

> "In the New England area there's a pretty strong country circuit, and it was five sets a night, sometimes behind the chicken wire. If they liked you they threw full beer bottles, and if they didn't they threw empties." **Reeves Gabrels.**

WORKING OUT SOLOS FROM RECORDS

"John Mayall came back from the States and he said to me 'I've got something here for you, listen to this,' and he played me two tracks of BB King playing in this little night club somewhere in America, and he was playing 'Need Your Love So Bad' and 'Worried Dream'. I used to play 'Worried Dream' as well, but recorded 'Need Your Love…' It was just the way BB King played it. Really beautiful." **Peter Green.**

In the previous chapter we looked at a method of building a solo from scratch, and the work you've done in this area will hopefully help you to develop an instinct for music which will grow naturally. I've always believed in a more free-range, organic attitude towards teaching guitar. Factory-farming techniques cannot be applied universally in this business. Teach 20 people the same things and you end up with 20 people all knowing the same things. Try to arouse curiosity and encourage individuality in those same 20 people and you end up with 20 individuals. It's a "for better, for worse" attitude, perhaps, but I find it more honest.

One thing is for sure, however: at some point you'll need some input, and for that you'll have to learn how to steal licks from other players. Actually, maybe steal is too strong a word – *borrow* sounds a little better, but the process is exactly the same.

I've interviewed and talked to hundreds of players, and they all seemed to have learned in the same way. Let's take a few examples…

"I had to just listen to the record, and if I missed it I missed it, and unless I had the whole record I just kept slipping the needle back until I got something similar to it. That's what made it so hard for me. But these young kids now can buy a video and watch it over and over again! I had nobody to tune my guitar and I couldn't watch the television to see what the guy was doing. I had to try to figure out *what he was doing! I just*

had to imagine what he was doing, and that's very much different to what you've got today." **Buddy Guy.**

"Everybody in my street had a guitar, and all we did was listen to the radio and try to steal everything we could. Also, my parents had a great record collection when I was coming up, and it wasn't until I started hanging out with some of my friends, when I went to high school at about 15 or 16 years old, that I went back to my parents' record collection. At that age, I had some friends who were listening to Buddy Guy and BB King, and so we started hanging out together and listening to their records, and it all went from there." **Robert Cray.**

"[I] ran into a record store owner who had one of the most fabulous record collections of pre-war blues I think I've ever seen. I just dove into that for about a year and listened exclusively to blues. For a while it was about just trying to find out what they were doing, but I would say that I just gave up trying to physically clone stuff. I discovered that, for me, osmosis worked better! I just basically listened, and I knew that sooner or later everything would just come back in my playing, and that's basically what happened. I gave up ruining records trying to work out every note Robert Johnson played, but during the years all of this listening has really started to come back into the writing. I think basically that that's the way to go." **Eric Bibb.**

"Eventually, just by listening to the records, you could tell what tunings they were using." **Johnny Winter.**

"Get the sound in your head by listening to records. Find the music you really like, listen to it all the time, and then one day you'll be walking down the street and the record will just play itself back in your head. Half the battle is knowing how it goes." **Bob Brozman.**

I know that, when I've answered the question "How did you learn to play?" by telling people that I listened to records and tried to figure out what was happening, they don't believe me; but I don't believe that I had any special gifts. I was applying the three Ps unconsciously, and I had an almost insatiable curiosity to fire the enthusiasm I brought to the task. In fact, I didn't even see it as a task or hard work, and I still don't. I see it as a riddle or a puzzle waiting to be solved.

Of course, I didn't always work things out correctly. I had friends who also played, and we used to show each other things and argue about who'd had the "right" version, but sometimes I'd manage to turn my mistakes into something new. Sometimes not getting something dead right meant that I'd discovered something and taken it in a different direction – I literally learned from my mistakes.

I also used to watch players when I saw them on the TV, which was rare in those days – you really had to keep your eyes open to catch anything – but I can remember doing things like watching Joe Pass in concert on TV and being entranced by what he was doing. It really was possible to play melodies and chords at the same time! After the TV show had finished, I spent about 40 minutes or so with a guitar on my lap, trying to imitate what he had done. I wasn't quick enough to catch most of it, but it was a spark which started a lifelong fascination with chord melody and jazz guitar. This in turn led me to buying tutors and reading books, and really helped me a great deal in learning about chords. I'm not a jazz guitarist – even today there are still riddles left to solve and new lessons that my ear has to learn. (It's a musical problem. I've got the technique sorted…I think.) I play blues rock

guitar by instinct and inclination, but having it backed up with a bit of jazz has helped me out quite a few times.

What's more, I believe that learning in this way is the better approach, with the ear developing and leading the way all the time.

"If you want to expand your horizons, the best thing to do is to develop your ear. When your ear is superior to your fingers, you transcend… Whatever you hear, try it!" **Steve Vai.**

"I think that the order you learn things is important. The ears come first, and then after a certain number of years you can start labelling the things you've learned. For instance, you learn that this series of notes that you've been playing is now called a major scale. Otherwise it makes so little sense because you're labelling things that you don't know how to use yet and it's more confusing than anything." **Paul Gilbert.**

Taking a more theoretical approach is fine for some players, but I believe that it's not always necessary to know the answers to questions. I mean, who cares how long a piece of string is, as long as it's long enough?

"Some people are too theoretical, but that's their nature. If somebody's an artist, they'll use thought as part of the artistic process." **John Scofield.**

Daylight Robbery

So how exactly do we equip ourselves with a striped jersey and a swag bag and rip off other players' licks from their records? It comes back to how well you've worked on your ear. In fact, many musicians develop a lot of musical acumen by trying to work out music from records. Remember when we adopted the slogan "If I can hum it, I can play it" a few chapters back? Well, that has to remain very much in force here, too. Luckily, the CD medium is far more user friendly than vinyl ever used to be. Constantly lifting the needle from the groove and backing it up to listen to a lick time and time again was quite an undertaking, but the cue and review facilities on CD players should be of great help to you in your pursuit of lick thievery. You may even wish to explore some of the software which allows to you feed a particular lick into your computer and loop it so that it plays over and over again. It will even slow down the lick in *real time*, which means that the track plays at a slower speed but the pitch remains true. Luxury!

Whatever method you use in order to take some musical dictation, the central process is the same: you have to begin by tuning in your ears. If you followed the exercise about humming and playing simple tunes described earlier in the book, this process will have already begun; if not, I advise you to re-read the earlier chapters of the book which dealt with training the ear, and remember that even slow progress is still progress.

When I was trying to work things out from records, I used to start with chords. The first thing I'd listen out for would be the bass note (either the lowest note in the chord or the note being played by the bass player). At first, I'd hear it, try to hum it and then forget it by the time I had my guitar in my hands. (Dropping needles back on vinyl necessitated a lot of walking to and from the record deck. You guys with CD players and remote controls don't know you're born!) It was frustrating, but I found that I could soon sustain a note in my memory long enough to find it on the guitar. (Remember the exercises on the CD teaching you how to find notes on single strings? Everything coming together now, huh?) There was an almost insane amount of trial and error, and it used to take ages at first just to get a couple of riffs together, but practice and overall familiarity with the process paid off and things speeded up nicely.

I won't claim that I'm brilliant at it. Some of the guys who work at *Guitar Techniques* can transcribe solos or entire songs at sickening speed with deadly accuracy, but they've been doing it for so long that it's almost second nature. You don't have to get quite that good, just good enough to grab what you want and get out…unless you want a job transcribing music for a guitar magazine. Hey, it's a living, OK?

Even if you can only pull out one note at a time, I would still advise you to experiment in this area. Remember: listen, hum, find, play. If you work in this way you'll be developing your musicianship fantastically along the way, and it will

help you to learn things quicker, too. The difference between working things out from records by ear and following a transcribed solo (and it's an important one) is that, when you learn by ear, the music starts inside your head and not on the paper. Sometimes using a tab transcription actually prevents a student from developing important musical skills, and the music is transferred from paper to fingers without ever leaving an impression in the consciousness. Without this vital imprint, the effect of the lesson is diminished and the music is never really learnt.

> "I've definitely a specific vision of these guys who have worked really hard on doing really difficult guitar techniques and who, because it's taken them so much work, have just ignored other things. They have no sense of songwriting, no sense of context of where something might fit."
> **Paul Gilbert.**

Troubleshooting

Needless to say, you'll have to begin with fairly slow, straightforward melodies (which is the same reason we started with nursery rhymes earlier – all good, musically-uncontroversial stuff), and I can warn you in advance that there will be notes which will give you trouble. These are notes which you can't internalise, which you can't even hear properly in your head. Why is this? Well, you might have stumbled upon a note which isn't in your present vocabulary. If you're working with major scales, pentatonics and so on, you're only making use of seven of the twelve notes available to you. Look at this chart:

C Major Scale
C D E F G A B C

C Minor Scale
C D E♭ F G A♭ B♭ C

C Major Pentatonic Scale
C D E G A

C Minor Pentatonic Scale
C E♭ F G B♭

Here are the notes available to you:

The Chromatic Scale

C   C♯/D♭   D   D♯/E♭   E   F   F♯/G♭
G   G♯/A♭   A   A♯/B♭   B   C

In the case of the types of scales that we've been considering, you can see that we've by no means used all of the notes available to us – this would still be the case even if we changed key – and so there will always be notes that your ear isn't used to hearing in context. For instance, if you hear a minor scale which is outside your vocabulary, such as a harmonic minor (it's just a name) like this one:

C Harmonic Minor Scale

C   D   E♭   F   G   A♭   B   C

Notice the maverick? Instead of the more common B♭, you've got a B natural which is going to sound "different" when you hear it. Therefore, if the solo on which you're working happens to call on notes from the harmonic minor scale, it's

likely that your ear won't be able to track the different note at first, despite the fact that you're used to hearing the B in the major scale.

Don't be phased by this. Learning to hear a note in a different context like this is like learning to spell a new word. You may stumble a bit with it at first, and you might even have to look it up a few times, but after a while – if you find that you have a continued use for it – it will take its natural place in your vocabulary.

If you continue to apply the *listen, hum, find, play* formula all the time, you'll find that your ear develops well enough to incorporate all of the notes of the scale, and a great many of music's mysteries will be within reach.

> "I think anyone who studies improvising long enough will eventually find a way to get all twelve notes available all the time."
> **Pat Metheny.**

MEMORISING

"I had a really good teacher in high school. He taught me relative pitch, and I guess he must have taught me the right way because after a couple of years, when I heard something, I knew what it was before any intellectual wheels started turning in my head." **Joe Satriani.**

I find that sometimes people have a strange attitude towards memorising a piece. I'll give you a few examples.

I once took classical guitar lessons for about a year. I'm really fond of Baroque-era guitar music, and I wanted to learn to play it formally. I had been playing electric guitar in various contexts for years, playing jazz, rock and blues, but I wanted to learn classical "the right way". I also wanted to brush up my reading, and I figured that in this way I wouldn't cheat, as I'm sure I would have if I'd tried reading electric guitar music. I was sure that I'd stop reading and start playing in the same way that I had originally learned, by ear, so I'd go off once a week and sit in front of some music and learn to play it.

However, I found that I couldn't play without the music in front of me, whereas I could play a 90-minute rock set from memory. What was happening? I couldn't work it out for years until I took a good look at the way I memorised everything – telephone numbers, post codes, PINs, door security codes, you name it. I learned that, if I wrote these things down, I'd never learn them, I'd always rely on looking them up. If I never wrote something down, or if I wrote it down but relied on my memory for a prompt, I had no problem.

If I learned a song or a guitar part by ear, I'd remember it. If I had to read it, I'd continue to rely on the paper version – it never became programmed into my memory. Now, armed with this self-knowledge, I know how to go about memorising things: I learn them from the paper version but ditch this as soon as I can. It works, too.

On another note, at the office we receive letters all the time, and I've come across two that

are particularly relevant. One asked why we continued to put page turns "at the worst possible moment" in music transcriptions because having to turn the page all the time caused a lot of hassle. The reader went on to ask "What do you expect me to do, learn the whole thing?" Well yes, actually, we did! It hadn't occurred to this particular reader that he was even expected to learn the piece, committing it to memory. In the way that he was playing it he would never actually stop learning it. He would always be reliant on the paper version.

Another reader asked if I thought that he should memorise a piece or not. I responded that the decision wasn't mine, surely?

In general, I believe that the learning process is only finished when you can play from memory. My classical guitar teacher used to say that first you learn to play the notes and then you learn to perform them, and that's a thing I've never forgotten. He said that any attempt to perform a piece which was at an "immature" stage would immediately be detected by your audience, and your own experience of playing the piece would be an uncomfortable one.

> "You never want to play music that sounds like the lesson you've just learned. People are sensitive to that." **Joe Satriani.**

As to how you learn a piece, all I can say is that people are different; they have different systems for learning, and many of them work, and so one doctrine isn't going to suit everyone. If I were allowed to generalise, though, I'd recommend that you do without the written version as soon as you can. If you play from it for too long this can introduce a sort of dependency on the chart, and tearing yourself away after this is far more difficult. Ask yourself how you would go about learning a poem or a play at school. If the process proved successful then, applying the same sort of criteria to a piece of music should yield similar results.

Musical Or Physical?

You may be wondering under which category a problem with memorising should be filed, *musical* or *physical*? Well, it's a musical problem; if you can't remember a series of chords, or whatever, it's probably because you've never had to memorise anything similar. It's a learning problem and, once acknowledged, can be sorted. The thing to do is to imagine that you're developing a mental muscle. You'll get it in the end; it just needs work.

If necessary, begin with small phrases of only three or four notes, as you would with the first few words of a speech. You'll find that "serial co-ordination" soon begins to take over. This is something which crops up a lot in other parts of daily life. It could be something as simple as making a cup of tea; you have your own little ritual which you've programmed into your brain by simple repetition over a period of time, and you can perform the act of filling the kettle, selecting a mug, getting a tea bag, adding sugar, switching off the kettle when it boils, adding milk, stirring and aiming the spoon so that it lands with a splash in the sink (or is it just me who does that?). What's more, you can do all of this while you're reading a book, singing along to the radio, working out what you need to do in town, or telling the story of your perilous journey into the office. It's all programmed in. Have you ever found that, if you're distracted halfway through a process like this, it's difficult to remember where you left off? Well, that's serial co-ordination at work. One movement suggests the next.

Musically, you can get by on this (in fact, it's probable that the learning process nearly always starts off like this), but if you really know a piece then you can play it from any point – the middle, the chorus, whatever – with equal aplomb.

I'll leave you with this though. I've forgotten who said it. It might have been me, but somehow it sounds too wise.

Experience will teach you how to learn

> "Originally, I used to forget them, no matter how much they went through my head; but the more you do it, the more you remember. You just train yourself to do it."
> **Malcolm Young**, on memorising AC/DC riffs.

GEAR: KEEP IT SIMPLE

"I also felt the guitar became a different instrument when it was turned up to maximum and fully distorted – it was no longer a polyphonic instrument, really – so it seemed to be crying out to be orchestrated, and I could hear just what it would be like in my head. This is long before Queen, and long before Smile, which was the group before that. Then there were a few things that reinforced that feeling. For instance, Jeff Beck's hit 'Hi Ho Silver Lining' had a bit in the middle where he double tracked the guitar, and just for a moment it breaks into harmony. I don't know if it was by accident – I should ask him one day – but I used to play that over and over again and just revel in that sound, and I thought that, if you could get hold of that sound and make a feature of it, and if it were not just two guitars but as many as you needed to make a proper arrangement, the possibilities would be endless. So as soon as we got into the studio, I was on the trail."

Brian May.

There is a lot of panic about gear in certain quarters. At the magazine, it's not unknown for us to receive a phone call from someone telling us that they have so many hundreds of pounds to spend on an amplifier, a guitar, an effects unit or something and want to know what we think they should buy. It's an impossible question to answer, and the advice we offer tends always to be the same: try as many guitars (or whatever) as you can, maybe check out some reviews in guitar magazines and base your opinion on what you hear. Different guitars suit different tastes, and you'll have to experiment a little and consider carrying out some careful research before you buy.

If the technical side of things scares you to death and you're afraid of buying a pup, try to take along someone who has a few years of playing on the clock to act as your minder. As a teacher, I used to do this for pupils because it was as much in my interests that they had a guitar which suited them as it was in theirs. I didn't want their enthusiasm to wane because they were unhappy with their instrument, or worse still have their instrument hold back their progress owing to some kind of technical fault.

I think it's pretty safe to say that these days buying a guitar straight from a music shop wall is altogether a more reliable prospect than it used to be. Over the years I've seen standards in guitar construction improve dramatically – for instance, they're much better and generally more affordable than they were when I started playing – so don't fear that you're going to take something home which falls apart after a couple of weeks because it's probably not going to happen.

If you really find yourself with a serious option anxiety, there's no harm in looking at the gear used by some of the players that you admire and aiming to buy a something similar. You'll find that, a lot of the time, pro gear is more affordable than you think. It's more straightforward, too. (See 'Celebrity Gear', later in this chapter).

It's still true to say that, with guitar-related gear, you get what you pay for. Don't expect a £150 guitar to sound, feel or play as good as one that costs £500, but be aware that certain models on the "luxury" guitar market will feel and play the same as an instrument that costs half or even a third as much. Just like cars, certain extras cost money, and all you have to do is ask yourself if you really need mother-of-pearl inlays in the shape of flying saucers all over the body; will it make you sound better? Joking aside, keep your eyes peeled, ask intelligent questions, do the research and you should be fine.

Suit Your Needs

If it helps, the checklist I usually go through with students runs something like this.

Guitar

What's your budget?
What sort of style do you play?
Do you need a tremolo unit or any other extras?

The question of budget is an obvious one. As for style, a heavy rock player might want a guitar with twin humbuckers and a design with a bit of "attitude", whereas a blues player might favour single-coil pick-ups. It matters. Then there's the question of trem units, whether they're vintage Fender-style models, or the modern "floating" style or whatever. Gradually you narrow things down to a couple of models and then visit a store large enough to carry enough of a selection to make your trip worthwhile.

Amps

What's your budget?
Are you going to use it for practising or are you going to gig with it?

Once again, budget speaks for itself, and style also has a role to play in this quarter, but the way in which you intend to use your amplifier the most is the governing factor. If you intend to use it solely for practising around the house then it really would be a waste of money to buy something huge, costly and monstrously powerful. Such a thing has been likened to buying a Ferrari just to pop down to the shops.

If you want a small amp with which to practise, a 15-watt combo with a single speaker will work out fine. It'll be powerful enough to play with a couple of mates (unless one of them is a drummer), as long as sensible volume levels remain a priority.

If you want to get into a band, either for the occasional knockabout in a rehearsal room or to play at the odd pub gig or a friend's birthday

party or whatever, then you're going to be shopping for something in the 30 watts or above range. Wattage is one of those fickle things which defies understanding. What it definitely isn't is a measure of volume, so don't let some statistics quickly rattled off by a salesman lead you astray. I've heard 30-watt amplifiers drown 100 watters. It's a matter of design efficiency and electronic hocus pocus which we poor musicians can never be expected to understand, so I can really only offer you a few rules of thumb concerning amplifier power.

A paradox in the gigging business is that the bigger the gig, the smaller the amp can be. Why? Well, at bigger gigs you can count on being miked up and fed through a PA. Gone are the days when your amp had to address the audience directly, which meant that your onstage volume was the equivalent in decibels to a shuttle launch. I've played 2,000-seater venues with very modest gear, such as 50- to 100-watt amps with either 2 x 12 or 4 x 10 cabs (that's gearspeak for amps with two twelve-inch speakers or four ten-inch speakers in a single cabinet).

If you're not going to be miked up and fed through a PA, but you're still intending to play the odd pub or small club, then the main difference you'll notice is that your onstage volume has to go up a few notches. Even so, amps in the 50-watt range should be able to cope with this. Remember that an amp sounds best when it's working at about 85% of its power range, and so a 30- or 50-watt amp isn't going to need as much of a push as its 100-watt bigger brother.

Effects Units

What's your budget?
Why do you think you need an effects unit?

We'll take budget as read once again; the equation concerning what you feel OK about paying applies every time, either narrowing or expanding the range available to you. I ask the second question usually to weed out the students who want a new toy. They've got their guitar and amp and some spare cash – what to do? Some reply that they want something very specific like a wah wah pedal or something, which makes the whole thing a lot more simple – we merely have a look at what's on the market and base a decision on what sounds good and looks man enough to put up with being trodden on all its life.

For those who are unsure what effects do but, heck, everyone uses them, don't they? I merely say the following: there isn't an effect pedal on Earth which will help you play better. If they're OK about that, and they don't think that they're going to be getting the Holy Grail with jack plug sockets, then I tell them what's possibly going to be useful to them first.

The list always starts with some sort of distortion device, which comes as surprise to a lot of people – I mean, it's built into the amp, isn't it? However, most players need two different sounds, in order to play both rhythm and lead. The simplest way to achieve this is to set a palatable rhythm sound on their amp and use a distortion pedal to pep up the sound enough for lead work. It comes as quite a shock to realise that guys with thousands of pounds' worth of amplification still rely on a £50 stomp box for their lead sound, but don't take my word for it…

> "Well, I like doing rhythm and stuff and I don't necessarily want it to be too distorted – I have to keep it a dull roar – but when you want to kick into a solo or something you need that extra edge, so that's when I hit the distortion box. In any case, there's something about the sound of that distortion box that I like. It squashes everything and makes it really fat!" **Steve Vai.**

I don't think that anyone will argue that Steve Vai has a great-sounding lead tone. Now you know where it comes from.

Other enhancements that guitarists use which come in convenient take-home boxes are chorus, reverb and delay. This trio are all interrelated in that they are known as *time-based effects*. In other words, they all rely on some digital trickery which delays the guitar signal going into them and feeds it back into the original signal. This makes them sound fabulously complicated, and I do apologise, but I'm not inviting you to care too much about the technicalities. Just go out and try

these effects. Play with them. You'll soon be able to hear what they do.

Amplifiers quite often come with reverb built in, and so a digital reverb unit (which can be quite costly) might not be necessary. Chorus units are fun, and probably alter the sound of your guitar enough to warrant the £50-£100 you'll spend buying one. They're great for dreamy rhythm parts and for removing a little of the bite from a distortion unit if you use them together.

Delay is used on just about every guitar signal you hear on CD. It's an essential part of positioning a guitar in the mix, and it's used in a similar way live. It's easy to forget that, as a guitarist in a group, you are part of an overall sonic picture.

> "The amp is set to get a good clean sound. Obviously it's set up for the boost channel as well, but I'm going for a kind of glassy, compressed kind of sound.
>
> "Our roles in the band are very, very defined; Vinnie [Colaiuta – drums] and Sting have got the bottom end covered, Kenny [Kirkland – keyboards] has got his stuff covered, and so it's an EQ thing. We've got our own EQs in the band so that, when you listen to it now without the band, it may sound quite thin and toppy, but in the band it sounds fine. I'm really relying on the five-band EQ on the Boogie a lot. That's where we actually do the final bit of tuning for a show." **Dominic Miller.**

It's vital to keep this kind of thing in mind when you're setting up your sound to play live. You may have to use a sound which would otherwise sound quite inappropriate when you're practising by yourself, but in a band context it's a snug fit.

On the effects front, I would say that the only other things your should want to buy are probably a group of extremely specific sound enhancers, which take up various positions in a long list of non-essential items. For instance, you might want to buy an octave box, but you're not going to use it all the time. Just remember that there isn't an effect which you can substitute for some hard work spent learning your instrument.

If there were, I'd have patented it a long time ago and retired to an island somewhere and commenced auditions for a sizeable harem. And you thought that it was my ambition to play three nights at Madison Square Gardens…

Setting Your Sound

This is another subject about which we receive quite a lot of mail at the offices of the magazine. If there was one common syndrome that I would implore you to avoid it would be trying to set up your guitar sound with your eyes and not your ears. I've said quite often in the past that I think that guitarists should be blindfold when they fiddle with their amplifiers and set up a sound. I never look at the amp controls other than to identify which is which, usually starting off with everything in the middle and then adjusting volume, gain, bass, treble, middle etc by ear. No set of numbers is ever going to get you where you want to go, although they may be useful for some ball park settings. This is the reason why I advise students to practise with their electric guitars unamplified, because in this way you can hear the sound that your fingers are making, and you can introduce amplification as the last link in the chain.

Remember that the sound you want to play has to be in your head first before it can be transmitted down to your fingers. A good guitar sound doesn't reside inside an amplifier. There's no magic spell that you need in order to be able to produce a decent sound, and you can bet your life that any guitarist you might hear has worked hard to get the sound from his fingers right before he even considered which amp he wanted to use.

Celebrity Gear

When I was originally learning to play guitar, it stood to reason that I was a complete novice when it came to understanding the ins and outs of gear. I didn't know which gear made what sound, and it was all very confusing, so in order to educate myself further, whilst taking the "trial-and-error" route, I scoured guitar magazines and interviews to find out who used what and why. I used the knowledge gained to formulate my own ideas about what I should be saving up to buy.

I want to emphasise here that the gear that you use has much less of an effect on your overall sound as a guitarist than you might think. I've had it proved to me on many occasions that a guitarist will sound the same no matter what gear he uses. His sound is as unique to him as a thumbprint and transcends the mere wood and wire of the situation.

In order to provide you with a sort of one-stop overview of the gear used by celebrities, I've collated a list of equipment which I've compiled from interviews that I've conducted or from players that I've seen at close hand, so that you can form a few opinions of your own. Understand that these guys change their gear payload or modify it slightly pretty much every time they go onstage, so don't be too surprised if you see one of them playing something that's totally different!

Buddy Guy
Guitar: Fender Stratocaster
Amplifier: Fender Bassman

Steve Vai
Guitar: Ibanez Jem range
Amplifier: Carvin Legacy
Effects: Morley wah, Boss DS-1, SDE 3000 delay, rack-mounted whammy pedal and a volume pedal.

Joe Satriani
Guitar: Ibanez JS range
Amplifier: (in the studio) 100-watt and 50-watt vintage Marshalls, Peavey 5150, Marshall 6100, a Wizard and a Wells amp
Effects: Two wah wah pedals by Dunlop, Digitech whammy, full-tone octave and Deja Vibe

John Lee Hooker
Guitar: Gibsons or Epiphones
Amplifier: Fender Bassman and Rhythm King

Dominic Miller
Guitar: Fender Stratocaster, Fernandes P-Project with nylon strings
Amplifier: 2 x Mesa Boogie Mk III into 2 x 12" cabinets
Effects: ADA flanger, Boss compressor, heavy metal, chorus, delay and phaser.

David Gilmour
Guitar: Fender USA 57 reissue Stratocasters
Amplifier: HiWatt AP100 (several)

Effects: Boss compressor, MXR Dyna Comp, Ibanez CP-9 compressor, Digitech whammy pedal, Boss Metaliser, Pete Cornish Big Muff, Chandler Tube Driver, Rat pedal, Boss GE-7 graphic, Pete Cornish Soft Sustain, Sovtek Big Muff, Electro Harmonix Electric Mistress, Univibe, Boss CE-2 chorus, Tremulator, volume pedal, MXR delay, TC 2290 delay, Lexicon PCM70 delay.

Martin Taylor

Guitar: Mike Vanden Artistry electric and Gypsy acoustic
Amplifier: direct through house PA or through AER amp

David Rhodes

Guitar: (in the studio) Fender Jazzmaster, Steinberger twelve-string
Amplifier: Matchless DC 30 or Rivera Bonehead
Effects: TC distortion, Roger Meyer Octavia and Voodoo Vibe, Morley volume pedal, Boogie V-Twin, Boss Tremolo, Boss Octaver and flanger, E-Bow, a Roger Meyer upgraded wah-wah, Electric Mistress and a Matchless pre-amp

Francis Rossi

Guitar: Fender Telecaster, G&L Asat
Amplifier: Marshall (Roland in the studio)
Effects: Roland GP8, Marshall Guv'nor

Nick Kane

Guitar: Gibson Les Paul, Flying Vee
Amplifier: HiWatt, Peavey
Effects: Boss CS-2 compressor, Boss RV-2 reverb pedal, Danelectro echo pedal, Ibanez TS 808, Dunlop tremolo

Peter Frampton

Guitar: Gibson Les Paul, G&L Asat
Amplifier: Marshall and Ampeg
Effects: Yamaha delays, voice box, Leslie cabinet

Robben Ford

Guitar: Fender Esprit, Telecaster

Amplifier: Alexander Dumble
Effects: TC 2290 (delay and chorus)

Robert Cray

Guitar: Fender Stratocaster
Amplifier: 2 x Matchless Clubman 35 heads into 4 x 10" cabs
Effects: Peavey Reverb, Roland Space Echo

Reeves Gabrels

Guitar: Parker Nightfly
Amplifier: Roland VG8 guitar/amp simulation system, set to Les Paul Junior into Studio Lead setting into a vintage 4 x 12" miked by a Sure SM57 (note: these terms are all simulations that are included within the Roland VG8)

Warren Haynes

Guitar: Gibson 59 reissue Les Paul
Amplifier: 2 x Soldano SL-100s
Effects: Alesis Quadraverb

Tom McGuinness

Guitar: Fender Clapton Stratocaster
Amplifier: Fender Twin, Peavey Classic 50

Eric Clapton

Guitar: Fender Stratocaster
Amplifier: Fender Twin
Effects: Cry Baby wah-wah

Brian May

Guitar: Red Special (home-made guitar)
Amplifier: Vox AC 30 (twelve of them!)
Effects: chorus, delay

Jeff Beck

Guitar: Fender Stratocaster
Amplifier: Marshall 100 watt

Paul Gilbert

Guitar: Ibanez signature model
Amplifier: Laney stacks

PLAYING LIVE

"Once, when I played with Sky, I played my Les Paul standing up with a strap, and the whole crew burst out in applause!" **John Williams.**

For most of you out there, the only point in learning how to play guitar is that you'll be wanting to perform at some time or another. This might be just amongst you friends or family, in a jam session or in a local pub or club, or you might even have your sights set on bigger things. Whatever the level at which your performing ambitions lie, the job remains basically the same.

> "It doesn't matter if you're playing in a wine bar with a drum machine or if you're playing Wembley Stadium. It's still a day at the office." **Dominic Miller.**

Certainly a lot of the same criteria can be applied whatever the scale of the gig. We'll take it for granted that you've got your gear sorted out and it's all in good working order and up to whatever job you have before you. My own take on the live gear situation is to keep things as straightforward as possible, and in doing so to keep the hassle factor as low as possible. For the majority of us who enjoy a simple life, I would recommend that a guitar, an amplifier and a couple of effects units are all that you need for a modest performance. Of course, this needn't be the case if you've got a road crew running around the place after you. Yes guitarist Steve Howe is famous for taking a large number of guitars on the road with him, and he often changes between them in mid song – something which introduces its own problems...

> "It expanded my workload! It took me about two hours to soundcheck whereas everyone else probably had about 20 minutes. But it pleased me...I don't know what else I would have done for those two hours. It gave me a very productive thing to do. If I could prepare all my guitars myself – which I have always done, right from the Sixties – then, if they're right, I can take a lot of pride in that, but if they're wrong I haven't got somebody to lean on. Some of the guitar techs I had knew the songs pretty well.
>
> "It was only in around '85 that I became really adventurous and I played 'Roundabout' one night changing guitars about seven times! I think I did the same thing on the 'Union' tour with Yes. I enjoyed doing it. It gradually became more complex. I've seen pictures of me from one tour where I have two steel guitars linked together at the front of the stage. I had a lot of things to do; some of it was pedal steel, some of it was steel. Plus I had a huge pedal board and all these guitars. But it wasn't anything to me; it was a requirement. If I was going to stand there and play the guitar then it was going to make the right sound, and if a song required me to play a mandolin then I was going to play a mandolin." **Steve Howe.**

However, for the rest of us who enjoy a simple life, I would recommend that a guitar, an amp and a couple of effects units is all that you need for a modest performance.

Preparation

> "There's no such thing as being over-rehearsed." **Dominic Miller.**

We can assume that you've rehearsed with the band, too, unless it's just a knockabout or jam session. The key to successful rehearsals is to go in knowing your part as well as you can. The rehearsal is for the *band* to get everything sounding right *together*, not for individual musicians to spend time practising their parts. Going in to a rehearsal only having half-learned things is a waste of everyone's time and causes tempers to fray.

The other thing which comes as a surprise to people who are new to band life is that they'll probably play a lot of material that they're not passionate about themselves. A lot of covers bands pick up a lot of work through being basically willing to accommodate their audiences and offering a very varied set list. After all, you're there to entertain people, although sometimes there is more of an incentive…

> "You had to be able to play a lot of different things in the clubs or you'd get killed!" **Johnny Winter.**

Ah well, I'm sure Johnny would admit that it was all character-forming stuff.

Warming Up

> "I do need to warm up or else I don't have the flexibility or finger strength. I warm up by doing fast alternate picking. It comes partly from the elbow and partly from the wrist." **Kirk Hammett.**

Often when you do a gig you'll be carrying your own gear from the car boot to the venue, and perhaps helping the other guys in the band to carry in their gear, too. I'm sure that you don't need me to tell you that a lot of this stuff is very heavy, and that lugging it around doesn't do your hands a lot of good. This is all the more reason to spend a few minutes warming up before the gig begins. This could take the form of a simple routine of exercises which will serve to bring the flexibility of your fingers up to scratch. Run a few scales or any straightforward repetitive workout in order to get everything working nicely.

> "On a big show, everything has to be worked out well in advance and consistency from night to night becomes a key area. If you start giving the soundman something he's not prepared for, he'll take you out of the mix without any respect to your feelings. Irrespective of whether you're having a fabulously creative evening, you're out! And if you're having a real bummer, he'll take you out, too. So the trick is to be as consistent as possible all the time. It's the complete antithesis of a club gig, where the excitement of the moment is shared by people close to you. A big show is a big machine and you're a very small element." **David Rhodes.**

Whatever you do, don't try to do a gig "from cold". Everyone will agree that their fingers feel really loose and co-operative a few numbers in, but you'll need as much of a head start as nature will allow when you start the set. Spending a few minutes with your guitar will also give you the chance to check its tuning and other important things.

> "When we did the festivals, I was never accustomed to playing in front of 30,000 or 90,000 people, and I always loved small venues, but what I've discovered now is that I hate narrow stages – stages which aren't deep. I get kinda claustrophobic. It makes me feel a little like a rock guitar cliché! I tend to pace when I play – I walk around in circles – and if I can't make a circle, that's when I notice it." **Reeves Gabrels.**

Size Shouldn't Matter

One variable over which you won't have any control is the size of the stage at the venue at which you're playing. It doesn't take long to work out that the owners of most pubs and clubs tend to maximise the space allocated for paying customers, and this can mean that you end up playing on very small stages. In these instances, you won't have to worry about choreography. I've played at venues where if I took only one or two unannounced steps to my left I'd have had the bass player's eye out, and so for the most part you're not going to be moving around too much. To begin with – and for many of us it's going to remain this way – it's going to be a struggle to find enough space for your amp onstage, but don't worry; we all have stories about turning up at venues and not even being able to find the stage, let alone having enough space for our gear.

Live Sound

The rules for setting a sound from your amp that we looked at a chapter ago or so are contradicted slightly in a live situation. Ultimately you have to rely on someone else's ears and not your own for your sound to fit with the rest of the band. On a pro gig, you'll be in the hands of the sound guy out front and you'll be 100% in his hands, never hearing what the audience hears.

On a semi-pro gig, where you may not have a sound engineer or a house PA engineer, you might be relying on your amplifier to project the sound so that it hits the back wall of the pub or club. In this case, it's a good idea to ask someone you trust to stand at the back of the venue and tell you what he hears. I've played a lot of gigs at which I was very uncomfortable with my onstage sound, and yet people came up to me afterwards and told me that it sounded great.

The reason for this is that, as sound travels it gets mangled with everything it touches in the venue – people, walls, equipment – and so if you're only a couple of feet away from your amp you're not getting the true picture. Beware of this, and remember to pack an extra-long lead if you haven't got a reliable mate with a good set of ears, as this will allow you to stand away from the band and at least get to hear what the mix is like from a distance of about 20 feet.

Other than the above, the art of playing live is learned on the job. There's no substitute for experience.

> "Any good musician is learning on the bandstand, you know." **Robben Ford.**

Nerves

Everyone suffers from nerves before they perform – everyone, OK? – so it's not just you having an anxiety attack in the loo just before you go onstage. It's happening all over the world.

> "In the very early days, yeah. It was because we used to try and mount a very big production with equipment that was not at all reliable, and so we all used to have the feeling in those days of 'Will it or won't it fly?'" **Steve Hackett**, on experiencing stage fright in the early days of Genesis.

Nerves surface in different ways. You may find someone who is the most reasonable and jolly guy in the world suddenly becoming snappy and irritable in the dressing room. There is an art to allowing your colleagues space and fraternal support in these situations. The best bands have learned to acknowledge an individual's right to be a wonderful human being 80% of the time and a complete asshole just before going onstage. When you play that first chord, something happens...

Case History

I once taught a guy who had recently joined a band and was extremely nervous about playing his first gig. I could see that he was fighting a natural instinct to run for cover and phone in sick but I told him that his priorities were first and foremost to make sure that he knew the songs and that, if he did, to have a good time. Simple. So we went through the songs and the couple of solos he had to play, and I tried to give him the confidence he needed, although was aware that I couldn't actually recreate a gig situation in my teaching room. I gave him an extra lesson a couple of days before the gig and told him that he knew the music and so his main priority was well and truly covered. It was up to him to have some fun.

When I saw him the following week and asked him how the gig went, I was met with the broadest smile. "It was great," he told me. "One of the women in the audience jumped up onstage and tore my shirt off!" Don't you just love rock 'n' roll?

It has always been my aim as a teacher to see that people enjoy playing, whether it's just for themselves or for a pub full of people out for a good time. Learning to play guitar is a lot of hard work, but there is an awful lot of fun to be had with a guitar in your hands. This has to be your focus, or there's no point.

> "You're out there playing for people and you've got girls chasing you. Now that was real nice!" **Johnny Winter.**

Après Ski

One phenomenon which people don't even recognise as an acknowledged syndrome is a feeling of restlessness after a gig. I know people who have to watch an hour or two of night-time TV no matter what time they get home after a gig, experiencing the physical contradiction of feeling mentally exhausted but too wired up to rest. As far as I can determine, this is down to good old biochemicals, and one specifically: adrenaline. The same drug which controls the "fight or flee" response within our bodies also gets released during fits of excitement or exhilaration, such as being onstage and playing in front of an enthusiastic crowd.

There's not much that you can do about it except let it work its way out of your system. Even so, I think that it probably goes a long way towards explaining why a lot of bands get into mischief after they come offstage – but that's another story.

WANT TO TURN PRO?

"Music is such a business now. Unfortunately, it's become so tied up with big company thinking and with the advent of MTV. It's just machines and imaging and marketing, and it really doesn't matter if you're not a good player any more." **Steve Lukather.**

The decision to take music up as a profession is still one that can lead you into perilous territory. I'm certainly not going to try and put anyone off going for it, however, because enough people tried to talk sense into me when I was an ambitious teenager and it did no good whatsoever. I was lucky, though, because I have a job which allows me to inhabit at least the foothills of music, even if I've never had the chance to sample the rarefied air at its peak. My job occasionally allows me the privilege of having coffee with Eric Clapton, talking astronomy with Brian May and hanging around backstage with Pink Floyd, but I've always compared it to visiting an aquarium as opposed to being a fish. You get the chance to sample a bit of rock's *dolce vita* but only from behind the screen of not really being a part of it. I tell people that I've done a lot of the things that I set out to do, including walking out onstage in a stadium in front of 40,000 people, although sadly not with a guitar in my hands. If it sounds like I'm looking for someone's beer to cry in, I'm not; I'm really very fortunate to be a part of the musical landscape.

When I first made up my mind that music was the only career I would contemplate, the industry was still pretty much in its infancy. You got in a band, made a demo tape and started hawking it around record companies. If you were persistent enough (and any good) you might attract a bit of interest, and if you could deliver the goods onstage and were prepared to put the work in and travel up and down the motorways of Europe then you might stand a chance of becoming on of the rock 'n' roll élite. Even so, you had to be a born survivor; the rock world is famously strewn with casualties from the rigours of professional musical life, and those are only the ones you get to hear about.

Famous dead alcoholics make news, but there are plenty of unknown soldiers out there who thought that they could take it and found that the pressure and continual dashing of ambition was too much.

"You can't really get too far in this business if you don't tour." **Eric Bibb.**

Today, as Steve Lukather pointed out at the beginning of the chapter, rock 'n' roll is now Rock And Roll PLC, it's big business, and the way into its inner sanctum is an increasingly less negotiable thoroughfare. When Frank Zappa was asked what advice he would give someone who wanted to enter the business, he said that they should get themselves a fashionable haircut and a good lawyer – and that was back in the Eighties. It's even truer today; music and fashion are notorious bedfellows, as even the briefest of visits to MTV will prove.

The rock industry has grown so large now that it has left few openings for new talent, and even a lot of the established talent out there is resorting to the internet as a marketplace for its music. Although it's too early to tell what impact the MP3 revolution is going to have on the world, I hope that it's the revolution that everyone hopes. If it is, it will provide the opportunity for anyone talented to make a recording and sell it to people.

All rather bleak-sounding, that, wasn't it? I do apologise, but like so many I got into the music business through the love of music, not business. At some point the two have to collide, and it can be very messy when it happens.

As Darwin said, the survival of a species is directly proportionate to its ability to adapt to the landscape in which it finds itself, and if you've made up your mind that the music biz is for you then I would offer some advice: don't be too monomaniacal about things. There are plenty of jobs in music which don't involve being a member of a band. There's session work, freelance work, teaching and all sorts of other perfectly respectable ways of earning a crust with a guitar in your hands.

Of course, session playing is also very difficult to get into. Many have tried and complained that it's a closed shop, and to a certain extent that's true. The famous conundrum with session playing is that you need to play a few sessions in order to prove yourself to a couple producers so that they will continue to hire you. So how do you get there to start with? Two of the three Ps apply here: Patience and Persistence. Anyone with enough of both of these Ps is bound to find an opening eventually. Just be sure that you have the

> "I got into playing sessions at the beginning of the Eighties, just slowly but surely. I got into playing for TV, which led on to records and movies. In 1985 I did a session – just one more in a series of hundreds – where the engineer liked my playing and gave my number that very evening to the guys who were holding the auditions for Supertramp. Apparently they had just lost Roger Hodgson and were looking for someone to replace him on guitar. I had heard that 17 guys had already auditioned, but I went along and hit it off great with those guys and they booked me back then as a sideman. I did a couple of world tours with them and then it was put on hold. That was kind of it until '96, when they called me up and said they were going to reform the band and they wanted me to be a full-time member. They were going to do an album and tour, so we joined up again!" **Carl Verheyen.**

playing ability to back it up!

Probably the most vital attribute that you can possess in session playing is that of adaptability.

> "Being a studio player in LA means I get called on to play a lot of different types of music, from jazz to rock to funk to heavy metal to country to classical. On any given day you'll be playing those styles, and I really enjoy playing different styles of music. I really enjoy playing country music, for instance. I love to play classical guitar, open up a book of Bach studies and just try to play through them." **Carl Verheyen.**

That adaptability has to come from somewhere…

> "I got a gig playing solo five nights a week in a restaurant, and so I switched over to a sort of folky thing, with Jackson Browne and Joni Mitchell type of stuff. So I was busy five nights a week with my acoustic guitar, singing and playing, and interestingly enough it got me into playing a lot of solo guitar, because you've got to give your voice a rest if you're singing that much. That brought to my attention the playing of people like Joe Pass and the jazz guys, so when I was about 21 I immersed myself in jazz. I mean, I was so into it I practised eight hours a day, learning standards and Miles Davis tunes. I was completely into it for about six or seven years, to the point of not really playing rock 'n' roll any more." **Carl Verheyen.**

Tribute Bands

Another area of playing which has sprung up over the past few years is the tribute band. A lot of venues will book a trib band on spec because they know that they are guaranteed an audience. The hardcore legion of loyal fans of the real band will turn up just to hear their favourite music performed live. It's a brilliant idea, even from a business point of view, because you're providing a service, playing music that has an established audience and have (hopefully) a full gig diary to show for it.

Of course, being in a tribute band does mean that you have to sign away any pretensions that you might have of being an individual or of possessing a style of your own – you have to adopt the playing style and repertoire of someone else – but for many the chance to work in larger venues and on a more regular basis is worth the dalliance with schizophrenia. This is definitely a growing part of the industry, with the top trib bands like The Bootleg Beatles and Björn Again playing venues that are around the same size of those that the original bands did.

I've seen amazingly good trib bands and totally lousy ones. The best have worked really hard to emulate and capture the band's sound, right down to the last detail, and are only just second best to seeing the real thing. Consider the fact that The Australian Pink Floyd were booked to play David Gilmour's 50th birthday party. Spot the irony in that one!

However, being a pro in the music business has so much more to do with personality than it does with talent or chops. I know of people who are obscenely talented musicians but their characters are ill suited to the slings and arrows of the rock industry. They're too vulnerable, too easily hurt to withstand the crushing wheels of an industry which really couldn't care less about what casualties lay in its wake. If you can't resist the call to arms, though, be prepared to constantly re-evaluate your position – sometimes things don't turn out as you expect.

> "I started out just being the guitarist in a band. I was never the centre figure – that came later – and I always enjoyed that spot, being just the guitarist. I wanted to be the Hank Marvin of my time!" **Peter Frampton.**

PASSING AN AUDITION

"You just gotta hang in there." **John Lee Hooker.**

Auditions are difficult because it's easy to feel like you're on trial. If you have a tendency to suffer from nerves or self-consciousness then this is when you're going to have to be able to take charge and just go for it.

Auditions usually fall into two categories: formal and informal. Formal auditions might be in a hall or rehearsal room with the band (and management) present, and you might have been asked to learn a particular song beforehand to play with the band. An informal audition, on the other hand, might be a meeting with the band in a pub without instruments just to see if you get along together and enjoy the same music before you're invited to come along to a rehearsal for a jam.

Irrespective of the level of the band for whom you're auditioning – amateur, semi-pro or pro – things tend to run a similar course, and you'd be advised to conduct a little research before showing up. Here are a few guidelines:

- If you're hoping to join a band that gigs fairly regularly in pubs, go and see them play, make a note of what material they cover and learn a couple of songs (if they're covers, for instance) so that, when you turn up for the audition, you can suggest a tune that is mutual territory for everyone concerned.

- Make sure that you're absolutely clear about what the band is after in terms of personnel. If they want a lead guitarist with strong backing vocals, don't turn up and tell them that you can't sing. Tell them beforehand and let them decide if they still want to see you.

- Remain open minded as far as style is

concerned. Simply joining a band and playing live is good experience, no matter what. I know plenty of musicians who, at some time or other, haven't been particularly passionate about the music they've been booked to play. If you start off with the attitude that "I only want to play this very narrow band of styles", you're not going to work very often.

- Don't try to be quirky, fey and temperamental because you think that this is how sensitive artists are meant to behave. A lot of what goes on under the public gaze is staged for the cameras, while behind the scenes everything is coolly professional.

- Don't show off. Most bands would much rather employ someone who looks like they're going to be reliable and cope reasonably well with the music in the set than someone who is obviously eager to impress.

- Cover your ego with shin protectors, knee pads and body armour. Taking rejection personally isn't going to get you far in the music business.

Case History

I once went for an audition which, thinking back about it now, probably did me a lot of harm. I followed an advert in the convention of all unemployed guitarists everywhere and the band named a time and place for me to show up with my guitar. I took along my Fender Strat and a smallish amp to a normal-looking church hall type of affair, plugged in and set about trying to prove to these guys that I was worth employing. I realise now how much you are in the hands of your prospective bandmates. It's very difficult to take control yourself and say "This is what I do, take it or leave it." You have to play the game their way, in my opinion. It's only polite.

They set about teaching me one of their original songs, and I began to interpret it in my own sweet way. They kept hitting me with the same thing: that's not what the other guy (the one I was replacing) would do. Their former guitarist's ghost haunted just about everything I tried to do that afternoon, and I left the hall thinking that I might not have exactly fitted into his shoes but I had probably given a fair account of myself. They didn't call – I had to call them, and was told that they didn't think I was right for the band. I was a bit upset about it at the time. This was, after all, a criticism of my playing and musicianship, and apparently I hadn't managed to cut it. The material wasn't hard – it was a melodic pop that was quite conventional – and I had felt able to cope, but they gave the job to some other guy.

I reacted very badly. I realise that now. I took it as a knock instead of getting back on that horse and making some more calls and attending more auditions. It put me off, and it shouldn't have. Auditioning for a band can sometimes be just like a blind date; if you don't get along, it's no big deal. Just move onto the next date and take it as it comes. Whatever you do, don't take rejection seriously – you'll never last if you do.

Mind you, my audition wasn't half as gruelling as some…

"The audition was really funny, and the funniest thing was that I was really nervous, tired out and completely shitting myself. I turned up carrying my pedal board in a bin liner, really tacky, and all the roadies were very amused, so I got up on the rehearsal platform, plugged myself in – and I wasn't getting any sound whatsoever, which made me even more nervous. All this time, Sting's just standing there being cool, and I'm not being cool!

"All the roadies were looking at the amp and rushing around like they do, trying to find the fault. They checked the plugs and leads, they even changed the valves on the amp, but they still can't work out what the problem is. Finally, one of them came up to me, reached out and turned up the guitar's volume control. I thought: 'OK, I've blown it.'" **Dominic Miller,** on auditioning for Sting.

I always tell pupils who are about to audition for a band that I skidded on my driving test and still passed. The examiner was prepared to forgive a mistake because (I assume) he thought that I displayed some sort of overall competence. Bands are like that, too; although you're on trial, they should understand that you'll make the odd goof and should be prepared to overlook it if you're otherwise sending out all the right signals.

"Mike [Rutherford] had a cassette that he ran through some speakers – they had the whole equipment set up for me. I just brought my guitar, played a couple of minutes of each song and Mike said 'That'll be fine, I think you're the one,' and I thought 'I didn't do anything!'" **Daryl Stuermer,** on auditioning for Genesis.

As with everything, there are a few points of audition etiquette that you would be advised to observe.

- Turn up on time. There's no such thing as being fashionably late; you're just wasting people's time and earning yourself a few black marks along the way. It's quite likely that the band are hiring the place in which you're auditioning, and so your lateness will cost them money.

- Ask for a contact number you can use on the day if things go wrong.

- If possible, try to record a sample of your playing on tape and offer to send it to the band before you get to the audition stage. This puts the ball back in your court; you can relax and make a tape without too much pressure, and the band will thank you for it. Then, if they think that you're what they're looking for, you won't be in the potentially nerve-wracking situation of having to prove yourself with the first notes you play.

- Be prepared. Make sure that your gear is all working at an optimum level (new guitar strings, crackle-free lead and so on). You'll earn points for acting like a pro!

"I had an audition with the band somewhere in Putney, I believe, in their manager's house, and the next thing we did was come to this house in Devon. First of all we had a house up near Barnstaple, and we didn't like it very much so we advertised and the people on this farm answered and said 'Yes, we'll have a rock band!' and so we moved in for two months." **Steve Howe** on auditioning for Yes.

Over the years I've heard many audition stories, but possibly the strangest was when Jennifer Batten auditioned for Michael Jackson's band. She told me that she had turned up to the studio and was asked to play in front of a video camera. She played the solo from 'Beat It' and was duly thanked and subsequently offered the job, not meeting Jackson himself until rehearsals began.

THE FINAL CURTAIN

"You don't have to be black and broke to have the blues.
You can be Jewish and have nice cars." **Leslie West.**

I thought it would be a good idea to finish this book by looking at some final advice and insight from the players from whom we've been hearing throughout the text.

"I think the general thing is to practise as much as you can, play with other musicians as much as you can – especially drummers, because it helps your timing – and use your ears. If something sounds bad, try and figure out what it is." **Paul Gilbert.**

"Listen to the past. I've run into a lot of players in the last 10 or fifteen years who don't really know where it was coming from – they thought it came from Jimmy Page, or they thought it came from Jeff Beck, or they thought it came from Buddy Guy or that it came from BB King. Well, it comes from further back, and if you go back and listen to Robert Johnson and Blind Blake and Blind Boy Fuller and Blind Willie Johnson and Blind Willie McTell there's thousands of them that all have something which led to where it is now. The beauty of it is that you can take one of those things and make it yours, but by learning too much from the later players, you don't have that much opportunity to make something original. I listened to King Oliver and I listened to Louis Armstrong and I listened to Thelonius Monk and I listened to Charles Mingus and I listened to John Coltrane and I listened to Archie Shepp. I listened to everything I could that came from that place that they call the blues, but in formality isn't necessarily the blues." **Eric Clapton.**

"Learn to play whole songs. A lot of people just know one riff or something. If that's all you want to learn then fine, but if you're wanting to get where you can get in a group and jam then learn the whole song. I've played every Van Halen, Iron Maiden, Ozzy, Metallica song under the sun, but it was very good training."* **Dimebag Darrell.**

"I'd recommend a guitar school if you felt you needed it, but if you do go you have to have the right attitude. You have to know that you are an individual. What you learn you have to interpret in a way that is right for you. To simply copy the people around you is anti-productive… If you want to be a virtuoso, by all means don't be embarrassed, and if you want to just plug into your amp and slam out distorted, untuned chords, don't be embarrassed about that either." **Steve Vai.**

"People who learn guitar tend to place the emphasis on practising alone in their rooms with a metronome rather than developing their skills by playing together with other musicians. The first-generation jazzers didn't waste their time practising, they jammed together, and in doing so picked up valuable stuff like timing and phrasing." **John Etheridge.**

"If you commit yourself for one hour to the key of B flat dominant and just start working on lines to play on that chord, whether it's a shuffle tempo or straight, just set a tempo with a drum machine or metronome. It's a real good place to start. Then, as lines start coming to you, write them down." **Carl Verheyen.**

"Music is anything, any sound you can make." **David Rhodes.**

"Pieces of music have harmony, melody and rhythm, and some sort of idea that makes them go. The rest is just a matter of orchestration." **Frank Zappa.**

"What do I represent to young players? I have no idea. I don't know where they've gone in their heads now, what their influences are. It's probably nothing to do with what my contribution was. I have no idea…I was just lucky to be in the right place at the right time and very fortunate to have survived." **Eric Clapton.**

"I think I learned the hard way. It helped, doing a lot of folk stuff and solo acoustic stuff, and then having a duo, then a four piece, then a five and then a six piece and so on. Your ability to feel at home with a lot of instruments develops from the time spent in the driving seat." **Mark Knopfler.**

"I write songs, I believe in beautiful instrumental music, and that's my focus. If you want to ask me what sort of string I use or how many hours I practise I'll go through it, but that's not really what I do." **Joe Satriani.**

"Whether you call it an accident or luck is debatable, but if you are smart or aware enough to realise that you've stumbled on the relationship between two chords that you like, it's worth writing a piece of music to that. Every song has a sort of punchline; it's what some people call "the money", and it's just a question of recognising that. Then you build around it. You don't necessarily use it at the beginning or the end. What you really have to work on is finishing a piece of music, but at least you have something, and it's not a problem – it's a piece of work. It's like a mathematical problem; you have to find the answer." **Dominic Miller.**

"If I can think of a guitar part but I can't actually do it as well as I'd like to hear it done then I'll get someone else who can." **David Gilmour.**

"If you take your lyric and change the tuning or the instrument that you try the song on, pick up something else and try it a different way, very often it will dictate something else to you. Even a different string gauge can create something different. Very often I've found that, if I'm playing something with very heavy-gauge strings, you're not bending and so something else happens." **Mark Knopfler.**

"Playing with someone like Joni Mitchell or Miles Davis, there's this thread that runs through the whole thing, which is really just love of music, and it doesn't matter what the style or form is, the heart of the thing is always the same. It's like looking through a prism." **Robben Ford.**

"The way it would work was simply to hum an idea to each other and then play it. All of us played by ear, and we would just think of ideas really. You'd have a chord sequence or something that would promote a sort of melodic line which you would have in your head and you'd think 'I wonder if I can play that?', and you'd translate that to the guitar. Then you'd teach your partner – or whoever it was at the time – to come up with the harmony line." **Andy Powell**, on creating twin harmony guitar parts.

"The two-hand technique was great, but I don't think you can substitute it wholly for conventional technique." **Stanley Jordan.**

"Sit in your room just like I did and listen to the records of the guys who are your heroes, learn their licks, learn all you can about it. Get your chops up and just jam." **Dimebag Darrell.**

"Guitarists are by and large bad sight readers and bad ensemble music players because they don't have the ensemble experience that other instrumentalists have." **John Williams.**

"This used to be jazz, but I fixed it." **Jennifer Batten.**

"I was playing the blues, I guess, same as I'm playing now. I've just updated that same thing. Sometimes I wonder what keeps me going, but I do just keep on going. And I love it – I figure it must be God, or whatever, you know?" **John Lee Hooker.**

also available from sanctuary publishing

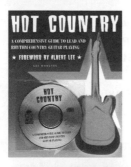